SCHOOL
COMMERCIALISM

Positions: Education, Politics, and Culture

Edited by Kenneth J. Saltman, DePaul University, and Ron Scapp, College of Mount St. Vincent

Affirmative Action: Racial Preference in Black and White
Tim J. Wise

The Edison Schools: Corporate Schooling and the Assault on Public Education
Kenneth J. Saltman

School Commercialism: From Democratic Ideal to Market Commodity
Alex Molnar

SCHOOL
COMMERCIALISM

FROM DEMOCRATIC IDEAL TO MARKET COMMODITY

ALEX MOLNAR

ROUTLEDGE
NEW YORK AND LONDON

Published in 2005 by
Routledge
Taylor & Francis Group
270 Madison Avenue
New York, NY 10016

Published in Great Britain by
Routledge
Taylor & Francis Group
2 Park Square
Milton Park, Abingdon
Oxon OX14 4RN

© 2005 by Taylor & Francis Group, LLC
Routledge is an imprint of Taylor & Francis Group

Printed in the United States of America on acid-free paper
10 9 8 7 6 5 4 3 2 1

International Standard Book Number-10: 0-415-95131-3 (Hardcover) 0-415-95132-1 (Softcover)
International Standard Book Number-13: 978-0-415-95131-9 (Hardcover) 978-0-415-95132-6 (Softcover)
Library of Congress Card Number 2005001983

Library of Congress Cataloging-in-Publication Data

Molnar, Alex.
    School commercialism : from democratic ideal to market commodity / Alex Molnar.
        p. cm. -- (Positions : education, politics, and culture)
    Includes bibliographical references and index.
    ISBN 0-415-95131-3 (hb : alk. paper) -- ISBN 0-415-95132-1 (pb : alk. paper)
    1. Commercialism in schools--United States. 2. Business and education--United States.
3. Education--United States--Marketing. I. Title. II. Series: Positions (Routledge (Firm))

LC1085.2.M65 2005
371.19'5--dc22   2005001983

Taylor & Francis Group
is the Academic Division of T&F Informa plc.

**Visit the Taylor & Francis Web site at
http://www.taylorandfrancis.com**

**and the Routledge Web site at
http://www.routledge-ny.com**

CONTENTS

Series Editors' Introduction

Positions is a series interrogating the intersections of education, politics, and culture. Books in the series are short, polemical, and accessibly written, merging rigorous scholarship with politically engaged criticism. They focus on both pressing contemporary topics and historical issues that continue to define and inform the relationship between education and society.

"Positions" as a term refers to the obvious position that authors in the series take, but it might also refer to the "war of position" described by Italian cultural theorist Antonio Gramsci, who emphasized the centrality of political struggle over meaning, language, and ideas in the battle for civil society. We believe that these struggles over meaning, language, and ideas are crucial for making a more just social order in which political, cultural, and economic power is democratically controlled. We believe, as Paulo Freire emphasized, that there is no way not to take a position.

The author of this volume in the series is no stranger to taking positions. On the eve of the Gulf War in Iraq, his letter to

President George H. W. Bush appeared in the *New York Times*. The words of Alex Molnar denouncing the war became central to the antiwar movement; he founded the Military Families Support Network and spoke to the nation in venues including *Larry King Live*, *Nightline*, *CBS This Morning*, and *People* magazine. More recently, his statements of protest appear in the new book *Voices of a People's History of the United States*, edited by Howard Zinn and Anthony Arnove, alongside the voices of other Americans who refused to be silent about injustices; Americans, such as Frederick Douglass, Emma Goldman, and Henry David Thoreau.

Alex Molnar is the foremost critic of school commercialism in the United States. Vigorously engaged in academic, public policy, and popular debate on the topic, his Education Policy Studies Laboratory (www.edpolicylab.org) at Arizona State University educates legislators, journalists, and the public on the dangers of commercializing schools. Molnar is regularly cited and interviewed in the popular press, and his book *Giving Kids the Business* was highly influential in exposing school commercialism and showing how it is inextricably linked to such policy matters as school funding.

His volume for the *Positions* series, *School Commercialism*, offers a rich history that explains the wrongs of this phenomenon. The book also addresses the new frontiers in the struggle for America's schools and shows what is at stake in debates over school commercialism. Not only are advertising, sponsored educational materials, and privatization initiatives undermining the public mission of public schools, but a growing public health crisis of obesity and diabetes is also inextricably linked to the commercial assault on kids, both in and out of schools.

Molnar has a distinctly American brand of social criticism. Rather than turning to theories and perspectives generated in continental Europe to analyze what is a characteristically, though hardly unique, American reality, Molnar draws on thinkers from John Dewey to Stuart and Elizabeth Ewen, as well as the rich U.S. tradition of criticizing commercialism as a threat to democratic ideals. Molnar looks to the architects of contemporary commercial culture such as Ivy Ledbetter Lee and Edward Filene to illustrate how the current glut of school commercialism in its various forms has been part of a broader, painstakingly executed, and longstanding project to transform American culture in ways that benefit industry at the expense of the public. If, as Molnar convincingly argues, school commercialism has been the result of policy decisions, then concrete steps can be taken and new policies enacted to rid public schools of the hucksters who hold students as a captive audience, robbing them of precious time and worthwhile lessons.

Kenneth J. Saltman
Assistant Professor, Social and Cultural Studies in Education
DePaul University

Ron Scapp
Associate Professor of Education and Philosophy
Director of the Master's Program in Urban and
Multicultural Education
The College of Mount Saint Vincent

The world is too much with us; late and soon,
Getting and spending, we lay waste our powers:
Little we see in Nature that is ours;
We have given our hearts away, a sordid boon!

William Wordsworth

1

EVERY CHILD
A CONSUMER

A plausible, imaginary day in the life of a child growing up in the belly of America's commercial culture is not difficult to conjure up. Marketing almost literally wraps around our child from the moment she opens her eyes. She wakes up in the morning after sleeping in sheets decorated with the images of Disney's Pocahontas. She brushes her teeth with toothpaste bearing the likeness of a television cartoon character. At breakfast, she eats SpongeBob cereal—a product brought out to tie in with the release of the SpongeBob SquarePants animated movie. Just the weekend before, she saw that movie, replete with product placements for Burger King and other marketers.

At home after school, she sits down for an hour of television, bombarded with pitches of or by Barbie, Bratz, and Britney Spears. For supper, her parents serve her Dora the Explorer soup from Campbell's. Last week at the store, she saw the can and, captivated by the label decorated with the icon of one of her favorite Nickelodeon television shows, demanded that her mother buy it. At bedtime, she dons pajamas modeled after the superhero costumes worn by the family in *The Incredibles*, another animated movie.

Throughout the day, this 11-year-old girl has been moving in a world awash with marketing messages. Not only her food, clothing, and toothpaste, but also her backpack and her entertainment are the handiwork of giant corporations whose mission in life is to make sure they are always on her mind.

It does not stop there, however. The books this girl carries to and from school are covered with paper wrappers promoting Marvel comic book characters—covers that were passed out on the first day of school in her homeroom. At school, she daily drinks at least one soda, sometimes two, from the vending machine. The machine carries all Pepsi products. Like her mother, she drinks Coke at home, but she's decided a sweet, fizzy drink is a sweet, fizzy drink, regardless—and she's begun to wonder if she doesn't actually like Pepsi a bit more now, and whether she might want to persuade her mother to buy it instead next time. A couple of weeks ago someone came to the school and handed out samples of a new pasta and cheese product to all the students, which she brought home and heated in the microwave as a snack before her mother got home from work. Among the books in her backpack are the last three she needs to read in order to qualify for a free Pizza Hut pizza through a reading incentive program at school. And in her purse are coupons for McDonald's she received last spring for a perfect attendance record.

Our youngster doesn't think about the way so much of her world has been shaped by large corporations and their logos, but besides the ones she sees, the trend has touched her life in countless other ways invisible to her. Her mother, concerned about whether the local public school is up to the job of teaching her child in the face of financial constraints imposed by a state legislature's freeze on spending, is mulling an inviting prospect: enrolling her in a local community charter school, managed by a big, New York-based company that promises to bring in all sorts of innovative new gadgetry and curriculum. Then there's the meeting coming up, advertising a new option—something called a "virtual charter school" that would allow her daughter to use a computer to attend school from home. Mom can't quit her job, but perhaps grandma could come in and supervise her granddaughter on the computer each day as she learns from home.

THE COMMERCIAL TRANSFORMATION OF CULTURE

American culture has become so besotted with material consumption that DeGraaf, Wann, and Naylor coined the word "affluenza" to describe the condition. They define affluenza as "a painful, contagious, socially transmitted condition of overload, debt, anxiety, and waste resulting from the dogged pursuit of more."[1] Just as type II diabetes is afflicting ever-younger Americans, affluenza is also marching down the age cohort. Clearly the imaginary child just described is at high risk.

The Oxford English Dictionary defines "commercialism" as "the principles and practice of commerce; excessive adherence to financial return as a measure of worth."[2] In *Lead Us into Temptation*, James Twitchell says commercialism consists of two processes: "*commodification*, or stripping an object of all other values except its value for sale to someone else, and *marketing*, the insertion of the object into a network of exchanges, only some of which involve money."[3] The Center for the Study of Commercialism offers this pointed characterization: "Commercialism: Ubiquitous product marketing that leads to a preoccupation with individual consumption to the detriment of oneself and society."[4]

One of the prime leisure activities of Americans is shopping. Every day and everywhere, they encounter advertising: on the sides of buses, on billboards, on radio and television, in the movies, on shopping carts, in toilet stalls and even in tattoos. Commercialism is pervasive, but, paradoxically, as the air we breathe, it is unseen.

Commercialism has become a linchpin of the modern economy, a force that shapes not only our work lives and our spending patterns, but also virtually every other arena of existence, and in so doing ensures its continued and increasing hegemony over culture. In her book *The Overspent American*, Boston College professor Juliet Schor documents how the consumption-driven nature of the economy reinforces trends in which people work longer hours, driving them in turn to greater and greater consumption—a phenomenon Schor has dubbed "the work and spend cycle."[5] In essence, Schor's argument is this: Western culture—and especially American culture—increasingly is shaped by the confluence of unprecedented affluence, abundant credit, and a pervasive ethic of consumption. The more we work, the more we spend—driven, according to Schor, both by the real need for convenience, to accommodate longer working hours, and by the psychic need to assuage feelings of guilt, resentment, or exhaustion brought on by the demands of work. The more we spend, the more hours we work in order to afford the possession-dominated lifestyle to which we have grown accustomed or to which we aspire. And so it goes, in an upward spiral of work and consumption.

In *The Conquest of Cool*, Thomas Frank chronicles how styles and symbols that were once truly countercultural and outside the mainstream of contemporary capitalist America have become co-opted and ultimately subsumed in the service of corporate marketing.[6] Naomi Klein, in *No Logo*, asserts that corporate marketing's dominance over culture has worked to undermine public space by encroaching on it with corporate branding; has reduced real consumer choice by the creation of "superbrands" that capture a wide range of consumer products under the umbrellas of a shrinking number of corporate marketers; and has distorted the world of work through the creation of jobs that are less and less secure and through the migration of capital to low-wage production regions, exacerbating the gap between rich and poor.[7] *Fast Food Nation* examines these trends in microcosm. In it, Eric Schlosser focuses on how the rise of the fast food industry has both been driven by and further driven changes in how Americans eat—with attendant effects in the health and well-being of individuals and of society as a whole.[8]

CHILDHOOD: MARKETING'S NEW FRONTIER

Commercialism has transformed American childhood and the institutions that serve children. As virtually every public space has become branded with the symbols of corporations that seek to sell products, services, and ideas to the public at large, children have become both a key market segment themselves and an avenue through which sellers reach adults. In *Consuming Kids: The Hostile Takeover of Childhood,*[9] Harvard Medical School psychiatry instructor Susan Linn describes the explosion of marketing aimed at children, and its impact on the culture of childhood. Alissa Quart, in *Branded*, examines the targeting of successively younger generations of consumers by commercial forces.[10] Schor has zeroed in on the phenomenon in *Born to Buy*, a sequel of sorts to *The Overspent American.* "Contemporary American tweens and teens have emerged as the most brand-oriented, consumer-involved, and materialistic generations in history," Schor asserts.[11] Behind that trend she finds "a marketing juggernaut characterized by growing reach, effectiveness, and audacity."[12]

Because the youth market is fragmented and those who measure it are numerous, with varied purposes, and interests in overlapping age cohorts, a definitive and precise accounting of how much children spend or how much adult spending they influence is hard to come by. Still, by 2004, Schor says, citing the work of Texas A&M marketing professor James McNeal, advertising and marketing expenditures directed at children totaled $15 billion—a 150-fold increase over 20 years.[13]

Whatever the precise amount, there is little doubt that, collectively, the discretionary spending of children adds up to billions of dollars a year, and that children also influence how their parents spend billions of dollars more. A 1998 review of marketing literature by Kraak and Pelletier reported that children between the ages of 3 and 17 spent $45 billion a year and influenced the spending of $295 billion more in 1993.[14] According to figures compiled by the Campaign for a Commercial-Free Childhood, children aged 4 to 12 made $30 billion in purchases in 2002, up from just $6.1 billion in 1989; children aged 12 to 19 spent $170 billion in 2002, a weekly average of $101 per teen; and children under 12 influence $500 billion of purchases per year.[15] Not surprisingly, the campaign reports that from 1992 to 1997 the amount spent marketing to children shot from $6.2 billion to $12 billion. Today marketers spend at least $15 billion per year targeting children.[16]

Children are, according to Professor McNeal, the brightest star of the consumer constellation. He notes that companies can virtually guarantee adult customers tomorrow if they invest in them as children.[17]

SCHOOLS: WHERE THE CHILDREN ARE

To marketers coveting children, schools, for many reasons, offer an unmatched way to reach them. First, children constitute a highly segmented market, with distinctively different characteristics depending on age, gender, and geography. Schools organize children by age, and are largely identified with distinct local communities. Second, schools provide a captive audience of children. Third, schools by their nature carry enormous goodwill and thus can confer legitimacy on anything associated with them—including that which is marketed under the school's roof and with its tacit or explicit endorsement.

Commercial activities in schools can be seen as taking three basic forms: Selling *to* schools (vending), selling *in* schools (advertising and public relations), and selling *of* schools (privatization). Selling to schools is a longstanding practice in the United States. Since before the first *McGuffey's Eclectic Reader,* private vendors have produced and sold to schools virtually everything they use: the textbooks for classes; pencils, pens, paper, and (today) computers; cleaning supplies for the janitorial staff; and food for the lunchroom. This sort of commercial activity has been and remains relatively unproblematic.

Selling *in* schools has been around for more than a century. It encompasses the use of schools by corporations to sell products or services, promote their points of view, or address public relations or political problems. As early as the 1920s, concern about commercial influences in schools was significant enough in the United States to merit the appointment of a National Education Association (NEA) committee to study it. The Committee on Propaganda in the Schools was charged with determining what propaganda (including materials from corporations, governments, and other organizations) was being received by America's schools and what policies or other mechanisms were in place to deal with it.[18] The report raised a number of significant concerns, including: (1) the decentralized nature of curriculum development and approval processes in the United States means that each school and school district must depend on its own, often limited, resources for evaluating the accuracy, fairness, and educational value of each sponsored material or program that is offered them; (2) the principle of democratic control of curriculum content (generally through an elected school board) is jeopardized by the abundance of unsolicited and unevaluated materials flowing into the schools from well-funded outside interests; and (3) sponsored materials and programs pose a distraction from the already crowded course of study required to meet state or local standards.[19]

The NEA committee's concerns remain relevant today. Indeed, the commercial pressure on schools is far more intense now than in 1929. Modern corporations seek access to schools in an unprecedented diversity of ways. Commercial messages, invitations to enter students in contests, proposals for exclusive vending contracts with soft drink bottlers, and offers of free equipment and services in return for advertisers' access to students are now everyday occurrences. Marketing to children and the commercialization of their classrooms are likely to continue apace as the "baby boomlet" enters and moves through school, as their purchasing power and consumer influence increase, and as other consumer markets and venues become even more saturated. Moreover, marketing in schools will increase, because it has been made easier by the education reform policies promulgated over the last 20 years. These policies have also encouraged the third principal form of schoolhouse commercialism: the selling *of* schools. Since the 1980s, there has been a growing movement in favor of privatizing public education, through such proposals as private school vouchers and the management of public schools by private companies. As we shall see, commercialism in schools and privatization of schools can perhaps best be understood as trends driven by many of the same social, political, and economic forces.

THE DANGERS OF SCHOOL COMMERCIALISM

Since children are generally understood to be a protected class, it is hard to justify marketing to them under any circumstances. Children do not have the same information and power as adults and cannot, therefore, freely enter into commercial contracts as envisioned by market theory. It is precisely their vulnerability, however, that makes children attractive to marketers. As McNeal notes, "Kids are the most unsophisticated of all consumers; they have the least and therefore want the most. Consequently, they are in a perfect position to be taken."[20]

Since commercialism is a reflection of larger economic, social, cultural, and political forces, whether or not schools and their students are subordinated to the marketplace depends in large measure on how we understand childhood and the proper relationship between adults and the children for whom we are responsible. Commercialism is not simply a threat to individual children. The commercialization of childhood is socially harmful. In *Born to Buy*, Schor outlines the extent to which much of the marketing aimed at children undermines adult and parental roles. Further, she reports, the rising tide of materialism in young people today is linked directly to personally and socially harmful outcomes, including increased smoking, drinking, and illegal drug use; a series of mental health disorders, including personality disorders and poorer achievement in school and in activities outside of school; and antisocial behaviors, including carrying weapons, skipping school, and vandalism.[21]

Marketing to children in schools is especially problematic because, as students, they are a captive audience and are asked to believe that what they are being taught is in their best interest. In contrast to schools, marketers are concerned only with buying or selling. Marketing cannot represent the best interests of society or of children. Thus, the effect of converting public schools into an arm of consumer culture necessarily undermines their essential civic function to promote the general welfare and strengthen civil society by educating children to meaningfully participate in the political, economic, and cultural life of their communities.

Marketing in schools is also destructive pedagogically. A teacher who hands out "supplemental" instructional materials that market candy, personal care products, sport shoes, or soft drinks is manipulating children for the benefit of a special interest and undermining the integrity of the curriculum. If lessons in nutrition devolve from material based on a serious professional assessment of what is best to teach, how it is best to teach it, and when it is best to teach it, to a "marketplace" in which any junk food purveyor with enough money to buy access can present its "story," all pretense of high academic standards is lost. Commercialism thus places schools in the position of ignoring their academic responsibilities and aligns them with corporations that in turn influence the content, tone, and tenor of what is taught. Paradoxically, despite the rhetoric of high academic standards, education reform policy over the last two decades has encouraged schools in this direction.

HOW SCHOOL REFORM HELPED PROMOTE SCHOOL COMMERCIALISM

In 1983, the U.S. Department of Education released *A Nation at Risk* [22]—a call to arms in the name of school reform. The report contended that America's public schools were beset by a "rising tide of mediocrity" that threatened the nation's ability to compete in an increasingly global economy. *A Nation at Risk* pulled together a number of criticisms of public education in the service of a single, more cohesive and unified message: America's public schools were failing, and unless they were reformed the American economy would lose it world dominance. *A Nation at Risk* helped to establish the view that schools were failing the economy, that corporations had expertise that could improve the schools, and that schools were hostile to corporations and needed to open their doors to corporate "partners." Along with business people who believed the rhetoric came self-promoting marketers, who took any opportunity to exploit for their self-interested purposes the pressure on schools to show that they were good "partners" with corporate America.

The decades following the release of *A Nation at Risk* saw a series of calls for more stringent academic "standards." Indeed, the report helped create the political climate out of which the standards movement grew. The standards movement in turn amplified the school-failure rhetoric of *A Nation at Risk* and led the way to market-based solutions premised on the assumption that the "monopoly" held by public schools was the reason for the alleged failure of public education to meet high academic standards. In the political environment that resulted, market competition became the preferred solution. Because vouchers were too politically unpopular, the favored market-based solution offered over the last decade has been charter schools—publicly funded schools created outside the normal public school institutional structures, and outside the purportedly "onerous" regulations said to govern public schools.

This policy trajectory created new opportunities for corporate inroads into public education. A growing number of charter school students, for example, are now enrolled in charter schools managed by private, for-profit corporations. Many of the same corporations manage and provide supplemental support services to conventional public schools.[23] The focus on high stakes tests to help achieve and assess the attainment of academic standards has helped ensure that public money flows to a "market" centered on improving test results, such as test coaching services provided to individual parents and their children, as well as to schools.

Thus, *A Nation at Risk* helped create and maintain the pressure on schools to cooperate with—and to be seen cooperating with—corporations. It opened the schoolhouse door to all forms of corporate involvement in schools, from substantive educational reforms to a proliferation of self-serving, money-making schemes. It laid the foundation for an approach to school improvement focused on standards and testing that in turn set the stage for the No Child Left Behind Act (NCLB) and its privatization provisions. For example, schools that fail to meet their achievement goals may use federal funds to hire tutors—but they are pushed to use private contractors, not their own teachers. Additionally, schools labeled as "failing" for five consecutive years are forced to either replace all or most staff including the principal, allow the state to take over, hire an outside entity to manage the school, or become a charter school. In important respects, the 2002 No Child Left Behind legislation may reasonably be considered the apotheosis of *A Nation at Risk.*

COMMERCIALIZED CHILDREN IN PRIVATIZED SCHOOLS

The trends toward the commercialization of childhood and the privatization of schools have, over the last two decades, become intertwined. The increasing commercialization of childhood has driven and enabled an explosion of marketing in schools. At the same time, the privatization of public schools, promoted by government policy, is transforming public education into a profit center for corporations. In many respects, children and their schools have become commodities traded in an emerging global marketplace.

Corporations market consumer products to the students who attend public schools and to their parents. Other corporations, in the form of test creators and test coaches, pronounce schools unfit to teach and proffer tools for improvement. Corporations operating charter schools sell alternative schools to the public, which pays for them with tax dollars. And world trade policies accelerate the deconstruction of public education into a collection of goods and services that can be traded in the global economy. As a result, public education, once viewed as a primary mechanism for promoting social cohesion, is being transformed into a vehicle for social dissolution. To the extent that marketers are arbiters of the condition of public education, schools must inevitably be seen and portrayed as failing. The nature of marketing is to promote dissatisfaction: Corporations create the itch, then collect the money from us to scratch it.

The chapters that follow detail the various aspects of school commercialism. Chapter 2 documents the trends in schoolhouse commercialism, primarily in the form of marketing programs in and around school. Chapter 3 reviews the marketing practices associated with the sale of unhealthful foods such as snacks and soda, and documents the harm such practices do both to the health and the education of public school students. Chapter 4 considers the very different legacies of three men: John Dewey, the progressive education philosopher, and Edward Bernays and Ivy Ledbetter Lee, the architects of the modern public relations industry. Chapter 5 examines the rise of public school privatization and the emergence of so-called virtual schools. Finally, Chapter 6 discusses the conversion of public education from public good to a collection of goods and services sold in a global marketplace.

2

THE SKY'S THE LIMIT: TRENDS IN SCHOOLHOUSE MARKETING SINCE 1990

In Georgia, a high school student is suspended and lambasted by a school principal when he wears a Pepsi-Cola shirt during a school photo-op to promote rival soft drink Coca-Cola—a prank that threatens the school's shot at a $10,000 prize.[1] In Indiana, students at risk of dropping out are enrolled in an alternative high school at a local shopping mall—where they walk the corridors for exercise, work at retail jobs, and eat at the mall food court between classes.[2] In one of every five school cafeterias, according to the U.S. Centers for Disease Control and Prevention, fast food purveyors supplement or supplant school lunch programs inside the school cafeteria.[3] In cities including Philadelphia and San Francisco, private, for-profit companies win contracts to run public and public charter schools—despite growing evidence that they appear to perform no better, and often worse, than the conventionally run public schools with which they compete for students.[4] A growing number of states have turned to other for-profit firms to run so-called virtual charter schools to provide computer-based curriculum children use to study at home. In many cases, these schools collect the same amount of taxpayer money as regular schools that must support a brick-and-mortar infrastructure.[5]

Public schools once occupied a distinct place in the culture of American democracy. The American common school ideal (if not always its reality) was democratic in ambition and purpose. It was part of the social fabric, yet set apart from mass culture, and as such was charged with the task of enabling and empowering successive generations to take their place as citizens in a complex, democratic society.

Today, across the nation and around the world, the ideal of the public school as a pillar of democracy is being transformed by a wave of commercialism. Commercialism is an expression of advanced capitalist culture and a profound threat to democratic civic institutions. Its impact on schools is, at its most basic, to transform the guiding ideal of public schools as centers of learning serving the public good to centers of profit benefiting private interests. Once held to be a public good that could be measured by their contribution to the community's well-being, schools have come to be seen as markets for vendors, venues for advertising and marketing, and commodities to be bought and sold. They are evaluated largely in terms of how effective they are perceived at preparing workers for corporate employers, and their mission has been transformed conceptually into a "service" that can be delivered by private businesses responding to the profit motive.

SELLING IN THE SCHOOLHOUSE

Schoolhouse commercialism is not new. Over a century ago a paint company in 1890 developed a school art class handout on primary and secondary colors that also plugged the company's products.[6] Sponsored educational materials have ever since been a staple of marketers who want to put a corporate message in the school. As early as 1929, the National Education Association's Committee on Propaganda in the Schools surveyed school officials to determine what sponsored materials had been received and what policies or other mechanisms were in place to deal with them.[7] The committee also conducted a review of state education departments' laws or policies governing the use of such materials, interview sessions with groups of teachers, school visits, and an examination of advertisements for sponsored materials.

In 1953, the Association for Supervision and Curriculum Development issued "Using Free Materials in the Classroom."[8] In 1955, the American Association of School Administrators followed suit with a similar pamphlet, "Choosing Free Materials for Use in the Schools."[9] Both publications were written to help teachers use sponsored materials appropriately in their classrooms. By this time, according to Sheila Harty, the characterization of these materials as "propaganda" had changed to the more innocuous "free materials." While both guides warned teachers against uncritical acceptance of sponsored materials, they recommended that educators not reject such offerings outright.[10]

In her 1979 book *Hucksters in the Classroom*, Harty describes the results of four questions related to teachers' use of "industry [-sponsored] materials" in the 1976–1977 annual Membership Survey of the National Education Association. The responses of 1,250 teachers suggested that approximately half of U.S. teachers used sponsored materials, and indicated that a wide variety of commercial interests were represented, including banks, utilities, manufacturers, and food processors.[11] *Hucksters in the Classroom* included an examination of many sponsored educational materials, a review of state education departments' policies, a survey of teachers, and a review of advertisements for sponsored materials appearing in education-related publications. In addition to discussing the ethical dilemmas inherent in sponsored materials, Harty also described in detail many examples showing bias, racial prejudice and sexism, inaccuracies, and incomplete or outdated information. In its 1995 publication *Captive Kids*, Consumers Union evaluated more than one hundred of the sponsored materials provided by corporations, trade groups, and others and found the vast majority were highly commercial, educationally trivial, or both.[12]

The launch in 1989 of Channel One, the 12-minute current events program that includes two minutes of commercials, has been widely considered the bellwether of the recent expansion of commercial influences in the schools. As such, it has been the subject of several studies on the extent of its use, its educational efficacy, and the financial value of the service and equipment provided. Critiques of Channel One's content include those by Fox,[13] Miller,[14] and Rank.[15] "Channel One in the Public Schools: Widening the Gaps" found that schools with high concentrations of poor students are almost twice as likely to use Channel One as schools serving more wealthy students.[16] Greenberg and Brand found that students who watched Channel One were more likely to express materialist values, such as believing that money is everything, or that a nice car is more important than school.[17] Fox found that student viewers of Channel One often could not distinguish between commercials and news content, and didn't perceive commercials as intended to sell them something.[18] More recently, a journalist's close look at the use of Channel One News in Springfield, Missouri, schools found wide-ranging opinions among students and teachers, while some school officials indicated a desire to drop the program in order to increase instruction time.[19]

MEASURING SCHOOLHOUSE COMMERCIALISM

There is no simple way to measure the extent, depth, and breadth of corporate moneymaking activities in schools. Firms engaged in school-based commercial activities may, at different times, have an interest in making exaggerated claims about the number of children reached (in order to attract clients); remaining silent (to shield market research and product introduction information from competitors); or minimizing the size of their efforts (to lessen the possibility of a negative public reaction). In addition, the varied and particular purposes for which organizations gather data on school-focused commercializing activities results in information that is fragmentary and often not comparable, and, therefore, not reliable as a basis for identifying overall trends.

The Council on Corporate and School Partnerships, an industry group favoring corporate involvement in schools, reported in 2002 that schools receive $2.4 billion a year from what the organization calls "business relationships" with corporations.[20] The council calculated that nearly 70 percent of school districts engaged in so-called business partnerships, and nearly all educators in a survey planned to continue those relationships.[21] A council news release containing those figures asserted that, from the vantage point of business leaders, "school partnerships benefit business and educators in four key areas: human capital development, community development, student achievement, and financial impact in terms of earning revenue for the business and providing needed funding for schools."[22] How those numbers should be interpreted, however, is not entirely clear in the absence of a commonly agreed upon set of definitions.

It is clear, however, that the range of commercial activities in public education is increasingly broad. In Indianapolis, students at risk of dropping out are enrolled in an alternative school based on the premises of Lafayette Square Mall. They attend classes, work at part-time jobs for credit, walk the mall to fulfill a mandatory gym requirement, and get their meals at the food court. Since 1998, America's largest mall developer, the Simon Property Group, has been opening alternative public schools in malls through its nonprofit Simon Youth Foundation in partnership with local public school systems. By 2004, Simon had opened nineteen such Education Resource Centers (ERCs) in eleven states.[23] The stated goal was to reengage students who might be lost entirely to the public school system, in part by teaching them job skills.[24] Psychologist Susan Linn cautions, however, that a mall-based school poses an inherent conflict. "Schools are supposed to be good for kids," says Linn, author of *Consuming Kids: The Hostile Takeover of Childhood*. She adds: "If a school embraces a commercial enterprise or commercial values, the school is sanctioning them. ... A mall is full of businesses that want to sell things, and sell things to kids."[25]

Commercialism takes a host of forms other than shopping-mall schools. It is, however, a challenge to measure it. Lacking data sources that allow the direct tracking of developments in schoolhouse commercialism, The Commercialism in Education Research Unit (CERU) of the Education Policy Studies Laboratory (EPSL) at Arizona State University has developed a method of indirectly tracking the phenomenon. CERU annually counts media references to eight categories of schoolhouse commercialism in order to monitor trends. This research was initially conducted by CERU's predecessor, the Center for the Analysis of Commercialism in Education (CACE), at the University of Wisconsin–Milwaukee.[26]

CERU derives its counts of press citations by conducting searches of four media databases: the popular press, the business press, the marketing press through Lexis-Nexis, and the education press through Education Index. In 2003–2004, CERU added Google News to its selection of databases.

CATEGORIES OF COMMERCIALISM

Seven of the eight categories of schoolhouse commercialism that CERU monitors have trend data dating from 1990. Those categories are:

1) *Sponsorship of Programs and Activities.* Corporations paying for or subsidizing school events or one-time activities in return for the right to associate their name with the events and activities. This may also include school contests. From 1990 through June 2004, references in this category rose 146 percent.

Sponsorship of programs and activities remains the most traditional form of corporate–school interaction. Corporate sponsorship includes supporting general fund-raising activities[27] and academic competitions.[28] Corporate sponsors fund National Merit Scholarships[29] and individual scholarship programs open to children of employers or to entire communities. One that stands out for the amount of money it awards—up to $20,000 per student—is at Coca-Cola, which along with other soft-drink makers has also been the subject of close scrutiny for its marketing in schools.[30]

2) *Exclusive Agreements.* Agreements between schools and corporations that give corporations the exclusive right to sell and promote their goods or services in the school or school district, and grant the school or district a percentage of profits in return. Exclusive agreements may also entail granting a corporation the right to be the sole supplier of a product or service, and thus associate its products with activities such as high school basketball programs. References to such agreements between 1990 and June 2004 have risen 858 percent.

Exclusive agreements put products of one vendor on school grounds. The majority of such agreements appear to involve soft-drink bottlers. Possibly the largest such contract was signed in 2003 at the Hillsborough County (Florida) school district: a $50-million, 12-year pact with Pepsi Bottling Group ensuring that vending machines in the county's 62 middle and high schools would sell only Pepsi products.[31] The practice isn't limited to food and beverage vendors. Photography firms, for example, also sign exclusive agreements with schools in which they require families to use the firm's picture in school yearbooks and in return provide yearbook publication services.[32]

3) *Incentive Programs.* Corporate programs that provide money, goods, or services to a school or school district when its students, parents, or staff engage in a specified activity, such as collecting particular product labels or cash register receipts from particular stores. Media references to such programs have risen 75 percent from 1990 to June 2004.

Incentive programs include Pizza Hut's "Book It" program, which offers children free pizza for achieving certain reading goals.[33] Other rewards—for attendance, for reading, and for earning certain grades—include McDonald's coupons,[34] free concessions at AMC Theatres' movie houses,[35] and free admission to amusement parks operated by the Six Flags chain[36] (to name just a few).

4) *Appropriation of Space.* The allocation of school space such as scoreboards, rooftops, bulletin boards, walls, and textbooks on which corporations may place corporate logos or advertising messages. More recently, this category has come to include naming rights agreements that allow corporations to assign their names to rooms, wings, or entire buildings in a school or district. From 1990 through June 2004, references in this category have risen 394 percent.

Blatant advertising is increasingly found in schools. In December 2003, Marvel Enterprises acquired from Hearst

Communications Cover Concepts, which distributes book covers, coloring books, posters, and calendars laden with ads in 43,000 public schools. Marvel's goal in making the acquisition was to expose more young people to its products.[37] Growing numbers of schools have either made or implemented plans to raise money by selling ads on school buses, to be seen by the youthful riders or by members of the public passing by. In 2003–2004 alone, plans were approved or proposals made in Lee County, Florida;[38] Braintree, Beverly, and Plymouth, Massachusetts;[39] Lake Oswego, Oregon;[40] Tulsa, Oklahoma;[41] and Miami-Dade County, Florida,[42] among other communities. Some schools permit advertising in the form of product-sampling. For example, in the fall of 2002, Unilever Best Foods sent home Ragu brand microwave-ready pasta dishes with students, anticipating that students would consume them as after-school snacks.[43]

Still another form of appropriation of space involves the sale of naming rights. A Brooklawn, New Jersey, school district helped pioneer the sale of school facility naming rights in 2001 by naming a gym for a local supermarket, a practice widely imitated across the country.[44]

5) *Sponsored Educational Materials.* Materials supplied by corporations or trade associations that claim to have an instructional content. References in this category have risen 1,038 percent from 1990 through June 2004.

A large number of corporate-sponsored curriculum programs have come to light over the years. Lifetime Learning Systems bills itself as the largest marketer and producer of corporate-sponsored teaching aids, boasting on its corporate Web site that it "knows how to link a sponsor's message to curriculum standards and create a powerful presence for your message in America's classrooms, with informative and engaging materials."[45] Writing in the *Irish Times*, one critic commented, "The purpose of these publications is not to open children's minds but to fulfill marketing objectives resulting in reported widespread bias in the content of the learning material."[46]

Some programs appear to be little more than advertising, such as the "*Elf* study guides in the shape of toys"[47] that were distributed to ten thousand schools by New Line Cinema in advance of the release of its film *Elf* in late 2003. Other programs may impart some genuine value—along with free advertising for the sponsor. In Florida, BankAtlantic distributed a math workbook to elementary school students with math problems with a banking theme—not incidentally building name recognition with the youngsters.[48] Court TV's "Forensics in the Classroom" curriculum, a trade publication noted approvingly, "built public support for science in schools—and won itself millions of brand impressions."[49]

"Pick Protein," a joint curriculum "to teach students in grades 9–12 about choosing a healthy lifestyle,"[50] is distributed by the Weekly Reader Corp. and cosponsored by America's Pork Producers, the pork industry trade association. (From 1991 to 1999, Weekly Reader Corp. was a unit of K-III Communications Corp.; the same company, now called Primedia, owns the in-school television network Channel One.) The Weekly Reader/Pork Producers curriculum "encourages students to consider what they eat, and to make informed choices, including lean protein sources such as pork, as an important part of a healthy lifestyle."[51] McDonald's free elementary school nutrition program "What's on Your Plate?" purports to teach "the importance of physical activity and making smart food choices."[52]

6) *Electronic Marketing.* The provision of electronic programming or equipment in return for the right to advertise to students or their families and community members in school or when they contact the school or district. Overall, electronic marketing references were 9 percent higher in July 2003–2004 than in the 1990 period. The relatively small increase, however, masks more dramatic swings in the number of references logged during the intervening years.

The most prominent example of school-based electronic marketing to children is Channel One Network, owned by Primedia Corp., which distributes thousands of dollars worth of television equipment that schools may use without charge under the condition that students be required to watch a daily twelve-minute news program, including two minutes of commercials. Channel One currently claims to reach about 8 million students in 370,000 classrooms in 12,000 schools.[53]

Electronic marketing takes other forms as well. One is Cable TV's "Cable in the Classroom," which makes the content of various cable TV networks available for free to schools, along with a wide range of in-school programming offered by individual cable channels.[54] Computer equipment and Internet access are another key vehicle for electronic marketing in schools. One example is found in Philadelphia, where plans were announced in 2003 for taxpayers to pay $46 million for a so-called state-of-the-art high school in a partnership with Microsoft, which is providing software, services, consulting, and support staff.[55]

7) *Privatization.* Management of schools or school programs by private, for-profit corporations, or other nonpublic entities. Although references in this category have been declining in recent years, the number recorded in the 2003–2004 study exceeded the number recorded for 1990 by 2,213 percent. The principal manifestation of privatization is in the use of for-profit corporations to manage public charter schools and, to a lesser extent, conventional public schools. This subject is dealt with in greater depth in Chapter 5.

8) *Fund-Raising.* Programs linking schools or school-affiliated volunteer groups, such as Parent-Teacher Associations, with businesses to sell products or services in order to raise money for schools. This category was first included in the CERU/CACE studies in 1999–2000. Retrospective studies have not been conducted to determine the number of references in the years before 1999. While fund-raising references rose 21 percent

from 2002–2003 to 2003–2004, to a total of 1,175, the number is still down from 1,772, the 1999–2000 total. It is not known if this is a real decline or the result of changes in search terms made in 2003–2004.

Fund-raising creates a wide range of opportunities for corporations to gain access to public school students and their families, and for corporations to profit from the "halo effect" of associating with schools. Campbell's Labels for Education—now more than 30 years old—and General Mills' Box Tops for Education are the two mostly widely known rewards programs. Schools readily encourage parents and neighbors to purchase the companies' products so that the appropriate labels or box tops can be collected in order to be redeemed for rewards.[56] While fund-raising was once thought of as mainly a vehicle for supporting extracurricular activities such as bands, drama clubs, or sports teams, a poll of parents for the National Parent Teacher Association found that 68 percent of schools that conducted fund-raising used proceeds to pay for "such basic needs as classroom equipment, textbooks, and school supplies," while half of the parents polled said the money was used to pay for "items normally covered by state funding."[57] Interestingly, the poll was cosponsored by QSP Reader's Digest, which conducts fund-raising magazine sales in schools.[58]

Broadly, CERU's annual studies have found a steady increase in the number of media citations related to commercial activities in schools. This may in part reflect increased criticism of and resistance to schoolhouse commercialism by community members, activists, and legislators.

THE SPREAD OF SCHOOLHOUSE COMMERCIALISM OUTSIDE THE UNITED STATES

Schoolhouse marketing is far from a uniquely American practice. Since the early 1990s, the Netherlands has allowed schoolhouse advertising, and by the late 1990s other European nations had followed suit.[59] In Germany, for instance, schools were featuring ads from companies such as Coca-Cola, Columbia TriStar, L'Oreal, and others as far back as 1998. At the time, Spread Blue Media Group, the agency with the leading market share in German in-school advertising, estimated that German students commanded $20 billion in purchasing power.[60] In London, Imagination for School Media Marketing put up advertisements in school hallways, gyms, and dining halls of three hundred schools, and each of those schools collected £$5000 per year.[61] The Campbell's Labels for Education program, launched in 1973 in the United States,[62] spread to Canada in 1998, promoted with a "Campbell's Race to the Finish Line Contest." The Canadian school that submitted the most labels won a "digital multimedia production suite" or a "schoolyard palace." Beaverlodge Elementary School of Winnipeg, Manitoba, won the contest, turning in 27,999 labels—almost 100 labels per student,[63] a lot of soup by anyone's standard.

As commercial practices have continued to spread abroad, not all have succeeded. An attempt in Canada during the late 1990s to establish Youth News Network, a daily 12½-minute current events program with commercials modeled after Channel One,[64] largely floundered. By 2001, a Canadian teachers union asserted that "the majority of provinces have now been declared YNN-free zones."[65] On the other hand, some international developments were arguably on the cutting edge, outpacing practices in the United States. In what at the time looked like an extreme example of school commercialism, a school in Auckland, New Zealand, took steps in 1999 to sell naming rights to each of its six classrooms for $3,000 per year.[66] For $15,000, a sponsor could buy the rights to the school's name, and all sponsors would be guaranteed product exclusivity and advertising rights at school events and in school publications.[67]

As schoolhouse commercialism abroad has mirrored that in the United States, so too has the international reaction against it. From Calgary, Alberta, in Canada to Nelson, New Zealand, proposals to name schools for corporate sponsors have met with displeasure and criticism.[68] In Saskatchewan in 2003, a 20-year-old newspaper columnist lamented the annual practice of enlisting students to sell entertainment books carrying discount coupons in order to raise funds for public schools, with a pizza party going to the classroom selling the most books: "There's a term for that: 'bribery.'"[69] The *Ottawa Citizen* editorialized in 2003 against vending machines and exclusive soft drink agreements in schools: "These schools are responsible for the welfare of children: They should not treat those children as a captive market for a particular brand."[70]

WHAT DRIVES COMMERCIALISM

While the commercializing of schools reflects larger cultural trends, it is also a function of the particular vulnerability of schools. Schools experience strong demands for academic improvement from parents, the business community, and government agencies. At the same time, their budgets are restricted even as they are under considerable pressure to, among other things, offer a wide variety of sophisticated and expensive technology to students.[71] These intense external pressures make commercialized offers of assistance, if not necessarily attractive, at least politically convenient.

One of earliest "corporate partnership" programs in the country was launched by Colorado Springs District 11 in 1993 to raise money for musical instruments, computers, and staff training. In 1996–1997, the program, coordinated by DD Marketing of Pueblo, Colorado, raised $140,000 for the district by selling advertising space on the side of school buses and in school hallways to 29 companies. Asked about the Colorado Springs program, June Million, director of public information at the National Association of Elementary School Principals, said in 1997, "I think it's going too far. But it's difficult for me to point a finger at schools and say that it's wrong because they don't have the budgets."[72] Christine Smith, director of community partnerships and enterprise activity for Denver Public Schools, was more blunt: "I got tired of begging for money all the time."[73]

The story of Colorado Springs is in many ways the paradigm. Schools seek corporate money because they find themselves unable to meet the demands of their daily tasks relying solely on the resources available to them from traditional means: local, state, and federal tax dollars. "First and foremost, our schools are struggling. Many districts are engaged in this [commercialism] because of the dire straits they're in," said Dan Fuller, a National School Boards Association spokesman, in a 2004 interview with the Associated Press. "This presents a real opportunity and a trend that will continue and possibly grow."[74]

FILLING THE GAPS

Examples are legion. Hoping to avoid a $900,000 cut to its $15 million budget, the local school district in California's Scotts Valley in 2004 hired a marketing firm to sell naming rights for a new theater or swim center.[75] Parents in Huntington Beach, California, threatened by state budget cuts, turned to fund-raising efforts in 2003 in hopes of preserving a small class size of 20 students.[76] Faced with a $600,000 budget gap, the Belmont-Redwood Shores Elementary School District in California offered to let businesses advertise themselves on a school walkway ($1,000 per brick), the library ($50,000), the science program ($100,000), or the entire district (price negotiable). While a member of the fund-raising committee assigned to implement the proposal called it a "win-win" idea for the district and its business partners, the superintendent of a neighboring district called the proposal "pretty troubling to me. . . . It would seem to me like we were advertising."[77] To meet budgets, a local district in Seekonk, Massachusetts, in 2003 laid off teachers, charged fees to riders of school buses, and sold advertising on school buses.[78] School districts from Santee, California to Beverly, Massachusetts have faced the possibility of closing schools to save money.[79]

Looking for ways to cut $1.3 million from its budget in 2003, the local school board in West Bend, Wisconsin, eliminated elementary school orchestra, cut thirteen full-time teacher slots, and reduced class time for art and physical education. Small wonder, then, that the school district considered corporate sponsorships for high school athletics.[80] In Massachusetts, a newly hired superintendent urged Nashoba Regional High School to look into corporate sponsorships for school teams after the school was forced to hike sports participation fees by 15 percent, to $328 per student, for the 2003–2004 school year. The fee was hiked because fewer students had signed up for sports—perhaps because of the original fee.[81] Indeed, a count in 2003 found that in at least 29 states, schools required students to pay in order to participate in athletics.[82]

INTERNAL CONTRADICTIONS

Educators seeking corporate donations often find tactical contradictions. In Washington state in 2003, school officials indicated increased interest in corporate sponsorship and naming rights in the face of tightening budgets.[83] Yet they noted that such measures would only slightly offset their costs, and they worried that corporate sponsorship could actually backfire if it signaled to legislators that it was possible to further reduce aid to schools.[84]

While some schools have been reduced to selling assets on eBay in order to raise funds,[85] other districts approach the issue more systematically, establishing permanent foundations to raise and disburse funds to supplement school tax revenue. The amount of recognition corporate sponsors receive varies. "Although they provide a mere fraction of the cost of running a school district, the foundations have become vital," the *New York Times* reported in 2004.[86]

Yet whether through foundations or more conventional means such as candy and magazine sales, media accounts from across the country suggest that fund-raising may accentuate funding disparities between wealthy districts and poor ones. For instance, school foundations are more likely to be established in affluent communities. Similar "rich get richer" disparities occur in even more ordinary fund-raising activities. A letter writer in St. Lucie County, Florida, complained in 2003 to his local newspaper that students who were unable to fill a 10-order quota of candy sales were excluded from a carnival held during school hours: "Why punish the poor?" he asked.[87]

The implications are increasingly grave as fund-raising turns its focus from paying for extracurricular matters to core educational expenses, as a writer in the *Seattle Times* observed in 2002: "When it comes to PTAs, the big money resides, not surprisingly, in the area's wealthier neighborhoods. With one PTA raising $200,000 in an auction and another struggling to involve parents at all, the disparity isn't between which school has newer football uniforms but which ones have lower class sizes, art and music programs, and new computers."[88]

CORPORATE MOTIVES

Corporations that market in schools do so with several goals in mind. Companies that sell snack food, candy, clothing, and personal care products simply want to sell something directly to the kids and establish the habit of buying their products. Other companies—computer manufacturers, credit card companies, even automobile manufacturers—are primarily trying to build a consumer base for their products down the line: They are building brand loyalty. "It's about locking in brand loyalty when kids are young," Robert Kozinets, who teaches at the Kellogg School of Business at Northwestern University, said in 2004, speaking about a program that sends children on field trips to stores at no charge to schools. "You get a lifetime of value."[89]

Companies often frame their motivations more altruistically. Nike, for example, gives equipment to schools "to provide opportunities for kids to fulfill their dreams,"[90] an executive boasted in 2004. Not incidentally, Nike—and other shoe manufacturers who operate similar equipment-donation programs—get to display their logos in high school gyms and get exclusive rights to sell additional equipment to teams and team members.[91] The man who founded Nike's contribution program, and has since worked for rivals Adidas and Reebok, sums it up: "It's a marketing ploy," said Sonny Vaccaro in a 2004 interview. "At the end of the day we've got to sell a shoe and a sweat suit. I found out a long time ago that the avenue to success is through the lowest common denominator—the high school kids. Everybody goes off the 17-year-old. They'll emulate him. They drive product sales."[92]

Schools are attractive venues for marketing activities for many reasons. The United States and much of the rest of the industrial world are saturated with advertisements. By some estimates, the average American views a full hour of commercials a day.[93] In attempting to reach children with advertising messages, advertisers must overcome advertising "clutter" to make their messages stand out. Compounding that challenge is the fact that children, particularly teenagers, represent a notoriously fragmented and thus difficult-to-reach market. For example, television ads may be a good way to reach the over-50 crowd—they watch an average of 5.5 hours of television a day. In contrast, children between the ages of 12 and 18, according a 1998 estimate by Channel One, watch television only 3.1

hours per day.[94] Advertising in schools helps marketers overcome both clutter and fragmentation. Schools are one of advertising's last frontiers. Apart from places of worship, schools are perhaps the most uncluttered ad environment in our society. And, since children are required to attend, school-based ad campaigns play to a captive audience.

The drive to reach children is fueled by the prospect of an enormous financial payoff. We have already observed how corporations covet the youth market. A 1998 Channel One study, "A Day in the Life of a Teen's Appetite," painted this picture of adolescents: "Teens are veritable eating machines, generating more than 36 billion eating and drinking occasions each year." This represents a rate of consumption that, according to the report, translates into $90 billion in direct and indirect sales, including $5.2 billion on after-school snacks, $12.7 billion in fast food restaurants, $1.8 billion at convenience and food stores, and $1 billion on vending machines. "The whole vending thing is absolutely huge," commented Tim Nichols, Channel One's executive vice president for research.[95] In the words of James Twitchell, author of *ADCULT USA*, for advertisers, when it comes to schools, "It doesn't get any better. These people have not bought cars. They have not chosen the kind of toothpaste they will use. This audience is Valhalla. It's the pot of gold at the end of the rainbow."[96] It is small wonder that commercializing activities in schools are proliferating so rapidly. And companies keep reaching to younger and younger ages. The latest target category is children from three to five years old; marketers are plying their preschools with branded worksheets, art supplies, and reading programs—knowing that by being associated with the school, they obtain an implied endorsement of their wares.[97]

A few companies that get involved with schools do so for something far more tangible. In 2003, the owner of an embroidery company in Bremerton, Washington, obtained free creative consulting for a new logo, slogan, brochures, business cards, and print advertising for his products from students in a marketing class at Bremerton High School, using curriculum guidelines from the Distributive Education Club of America.[98]

Still, the search for current or future customers tends to drive most such arrangements. Merrill Lynch & Co. almost certainly gains coveted early exposure to potential future customers with its fifteen-lesson curriculum and video series, produced to improve the "financial literacy" of students.[99] So, too, does the Rockville, Maryland, federal credit union that has established "mini-branches" in a half-dozen Maryland schools, where students can bank and work as tellers.[100]

SELF-SERVING CURRICULA

The use of corporate curricular materials presents challenges of its own. The efforts by credit card companies to teach "money management skills," for example, illustrate the contradiction of having self-interested corporations take on the role of protecting children from their own advertising campaigns. In 1999, the Consumer Federation of America released a study documenting the severe pressure credit card debt is putting on students and criticizing the marketing efforts of credit card companies aimed at college-aged youths. That same year, the American Association of University Women report "Gaining a Foothold" suggested that credit card debt presented an obstacle to pursuing or continuing a college education. It is at least possible, therefore, that the most effective method of promoting good money management skills among young adults would be for credit card companies to stop the seductive advertising campaigns aimed at college-aged youths they currently fund.

Brand loyalty is also a driving force for companies that participate in Chicago-based Field Trip Factory, which offers schools free field trips to stores.[101] Through Field Trip Factory, students visit Petco to learn about animal welfare, Toys "R" Us to learn about party planning, and grocery stores to learn about nutrition.[102] The stores, in turn, pay Field Trip Factory for the exposure and for coordinating the visits; a supermarket spokesman in Massachusetts told the *Boston Globe* in 2004 that his firm paid $24,000 for a 12-week trial at 24 New England stores.[103] President and founder Susan Singer casts her firm's service as providing free educational opportunities and teaching students to be smarter consumers.[104] But at least one Petco manager was frank about the objective: "We are getting kids in at a young age so we can educate them and hopefully turn them into customers," said Indrani Mukherjee, general manager of a Buffalo, New York, Petco, in 2004.[105] For H. E. Butt Grocery Co. based in San Antonio, Texas, Field Trip Factory tours are an opportunity to promote its private label children's food line, H-E-Buddy. The store also highlights General Mills and Colgate products during the tour, in return for sponsorship funds from those two corporations.[106]

Yet it's not clear that schools using Field Trip Factory are saving any money. They still must pay for the bus. Additionally, at least one Chicago museum spokeswoman said that the museum does not charge admission for school field trips, either.[107]

Some critics have been skeptical. "The job of schools is not to groom pliant consumers," editorialized the *Philadelphia Inquirer* in 2004. "It is to imbue children first with a love of learning for its own sake, then with the skills needed for citizenship and career. ... Schools shouldn't set up their students to be exploited. If they do, parents must object."[108]

But Field Trip Factory is not alone. Cutting out the middleman, Toys "R" Us has established its own program of organizing free field trips to its stores, rolling out the program initially in rural communities in Wisconsin, Mississippi, Texas, and North Carolina.[109] In a 2003 interview, Michael Rubin, the toy company's director of new business, observed that these are "not places with a hundred museums. We're providing a destination that didn't exist before to provide an out-of-classroom experience."[110]

From the company's vantage point, it's doing schools a favor and filling a gap. Others might wonder if, however, it is exploiting those schools' relative lack of resources; indeed, Rubin acknowledges, Toys "R" Us hopes to gain a competitive advantage from the experience as well: "We are learning about how people think."[111]

BUYING GOODWILL

Beyond brand loyalty, corporations seek opportunities through schools to build loyalties of another sort. For many, relationships with schools are an opportunity to foster community goodwill. When Target Corp. built a warehouse in Oconomowoc, Wisconsin, in the 1990s, community residents weren't happy, fearing pollution and an eyesore.[112] Writing in a magazine for school principals in 2003, Oconomowoc principal Joseph Moylan boasted about how the school and Target implemented a "partnership" program that has brought about a hundred students with truancy problems or at risk for dropping out onto the warehouse's premises for career development, alternative education, and part-time jobs—benefiting Target with "improved public relations" in the process.[113]

Corporations that have already been skillful in playing job-hungry communities off each other in order to wring concessions in taxes and development costs find that corporate philanthropy can, for pennies on the dollar, help soften local resistance. When Nissan North America won $363 million in tax incentives for a plant in Jackson, Mississippi, in 2003, the company gave $20,000 to the group 100 Black Men of Jackson, in keeping with its view of corporate philanthropy as "a key business strategy," in the words of one executive.[114] Next door in Alabama—where automakers have gotten record tax incentive packages—Hyundai gave $400,000 to a reading initiative at the April 2003 groundbreaking of an assembly plant in Montgomery, and Toyota gave

$500,000 to a public school foundation in Huntsville, where it has an engine plant.[115]

Lest anyone continue to think that this is primarily about altruism, consider the remarks of a chemical company executive in the publication *PR Week*. Speaking in 2004 about sponsorships of all kinds, not just in schools, Jane Crawford, of Pennsylvania-based Atofina, said, "I think there was a time when we would agree to sponsorships and not look for an ROI [return on investment]. But these days you have to get it. You just have to."[116]

Some corporate curriculum materials don't necessarily relate directly to the company's products, but are intended to promote a company's cultural values. For instance, MassMutual Financial Group and its Oppenheimer Funds unit sponsor an "educational outreach program" for middle school children, in use in 2,500 classrooms, that focuses on "character education" and offers "lessons on tolerance, body image, diversity, and teamwork."[117]

HONOR AND GLORY

Chick-fil-A, a fast food chain that articulates its "statement of corporate purpose" as "to glorify God by being a faithful steward of all that is entrusted to us and to have a positive influence on all who come in contact with Chick-fil-A,"[118] gives a "Core Essentials" character-education curriculum to 1,100 elementary schools around the country, reaching, by its own count, 575,000 students per year. The company also has incentive programs for reading and attendance in schools with which it forms partnerships, and gives out books on partnership with public television's reading show "Between the Lions."[119]

To be sure, for-profit corporations are not alone in providing curricular materials to schools in hopes of benefiting from the exposure. The Audubon Society's local chapter in Syracuse, New York, donated free "classroom kits" to area youth organizations, including schools. The kits included a newspaper for pupils, teacher resource manuals, subscriptions to the national Audubon Society's magazine, and local field trips.[120]

Yet corporate programs are, arguably, uniquely self-interested and driven by the need for a "return on investment." Parents and teachers alike should have every reason to question whether the Pork Producers/Weekly Reader "Pick Protein" curriculum provides a full, complete, and balanced appraisal of, for example, the health benefits of a vegetarian diet, or the conditions under which pigs are raised and their meat is processed. Similar questions might be raised about whether McDonald's "What's on your Plate?" program inappropriately diverts classroom discussion from the high fat, sugar, and sodium content of the fast food purveyor's products.

There are other examples. In 2003, for instance, the Motion Picture Association of America spent $100,000 to distribute materials aimed at discouraging music and movie piracy to classrooms for children in grades five through nine. "What's the Diff?: A Guide to Digital Citizenship" is a lesson plan that seeks to discourage people from free online file-sharing services with the message, "If you haven't paid for it, you've stolen it."[121] The program raised objections from civil libertarians for not addressing nuances in copyright law, such as fair use. "This is really sounding like Soviet-style education," said Wendy Seltzer, a lawyer for the Electronic Frontier Foundation. "First, they're indoctrinating the students, and then having students indoctrinate their peers. . . . The takeaway message has got to be more nuanced. Copyright is a complicated subject."[122]

A similarly one-sided "lesson" may be found in the field trip that U.S. Sugar Corp. paid for South Plantation High School environmental science students in Plantation, Florida. During the all-expenses paid visit to the U.S. Sugar refineries and cane fields in Clewiston, Florida, in early 2004, students "heard U.S.

Sugar's position that it doesn't pollute the Everglades as much as the media and critics claim."[123]

THE LIMITS OF CORPORATE LARGESSE

The justification schools use for entering into marketing relationships with corporations is financial need, yet the monetary reward is often very modest. As early as 1999, the *San Antonio Express-News* reported that school districts in the San Antonio area that had permitted advertising on their school buses did not realize the revenue they had anticipated.[124] An advertising program in Colorado Springs District 11 (32,000 students)[125] collected $140,000 in 1999—approximately $4.35 per student, hardly enough to make a dent in the $4.8 million that District 11 announced it had to trim from its budget that year.[126] A 2001 deal that named the Brooklawn School District's new high school gym after a local supermarket fetched the school $100,000—but over 20 years.[127] The school's annual $5,000 a year from the transaction was only about enough to cover maintenance and operation costs, the school superintendent told the *Washington Post*.[128]

If the revenue gained is relatively paltry, however, the damage done to educational integrity is more worrisome. Schoolhouse commercialism should not be considered as either innocuous or as only a relatively minor aspect of a larger pattern of cultural, economic, or political transformation. For example, while supporters of Channel One News see the in-class television program as a vehicle for encouraging students to get more in touch with current events,[129] criticism of its advertising range from complaints about pushing unhealthful junk foods to—in the words of one conservative Christian critic—promotions for "PG-13 movies packed with sexual innuendo, profanity, and violence."[130]

Marketing relationships end up subordinating the interests of schools and their students to those of the marketers. Consider the story of John Bushey. On September 23, 1998, Mr. Bushey, the executive director of school leadership for Colorado Springs School District 11, sent a memo to district principals. Normally, a memo from a school administrator's office outlining expectations for the coming year would not merit press attention. John Bushey's memo, however, attracted the attention of the *Denver Post*,[131] *Harper's Magazine*,[132] the *Washington Post*,[133] and the *New York Times*.[134] In his memo Mr. Bushey—the district's point man for its exclusive contract with Coca-Cola, or in his own words, the district's "Coke Dude"—pointed out that District 11 students needed to consume seventy thousand cases of Coke products if the district was to receive the full financial benefit of its exclusive sales agreement with the company. In order to better promote the consumption of Coke products, Mr. Bushey offered school principals tips such as, "Allow students to purchase and consume vended products throughout the day," and "locate machines where they are accessible to the students all day." He also offered to provide their schools with additional electrical outlets if necessary and enclosed a list of Coke products and a calendar of promotional events intended to help advertise them.

Mr. Bushey's zeal may in part be explained by his tardy realization that the district's exclusive agreement with Coke counted only vending machine sales toward the system's annual quota; Coca-Cola products sold at cafeteria fountains wouldn't count. In March 1999, Mr. Bushey told the *Washington Post* that the district might not meet its contractual goals.[135] In May he told the *New York Times*, "Quite honestly, they were smarter than us."[136]

Indeed.

The potentially negative health effects of marketing relationships with purveyors of junk food and soft drinks is detailed in Chapter 3. Yet regardless of the health problems brought on by soft drink consumption, Mr. Bushey's actions beg the question: What is it that we expect of our school administrators? Is it their job to do what they can to help students learn and achieve in school? Or is it their job to sell more caramel-colored sugar water?

CHALLENGES TO INTEGRITY

Lurking behind the cash proffered by corporate marketing programs in schools are constant tests of integrity. In 2003, for instance, a school district in Florida sought to get around a state law forbidding advertising on the outside of school buses by selling ads on the inside windows.[137] In Utah, corporate sponsorship of a junior high school by McDonald's—which led to flying a corporate flag on the school premises—produced a free-speech challenge. Members of PETA (People for the Ethical Treatment of Animals), protesting McDonald's, picketed at the school in 1999 and were arrested. A lower court upheld the arrests, citing a Utah law that forbade "interference with peaceful conduct of school activities." An appeals court in 2003, however, reinstated the protesters' First Amendment lawsuit against their arrests, holding that the state law in question didn't address junior high schools, only colleges and universities.[138] A newspaper editorial writer who weighed in a few days later defended the arrests, however, apparently oblivious to the free-speech issues embedded in the case.[139]

Putting schools in malls presents similar free-speech conflicts. Writing on the Education Resource Center (ERC), the school for at-risk teens at the Lafayette Square Mall in Indianapolis, Chris Berdik in the *Boston Globe* recounted how security guards questioned his right to take notes on the mall grounds—which was, after all, private property. Berdik talked his way out of a confrontation, but suggests that the incident offered "unintended civics lessons that might await students just outside the ERC's doors."[140]

Defenders of schoolhouse commercialism argue that it is no more than a way for schools to get needed additional resources, and that businesses should be thanked for what they provide and encouraged to share more largesse. Events in Oregon in 2003 brought into sharp relief the way business interests undermine schools even as they seek credit for their "contributions." On the one hand, a variety of the state's businesses, small and large, held drives to raise money for schools—drives that, not incidentally, were structured to promote their own sales: a car dealer gave $25 for every car sold, with a goal of $100,000; organic fruit purveyors donated 50 cents from every pound of fruit sold; and restaurants and at least one hair salon chain donated percentages of their sales as well. Yet the need for these donations was spurred in part due to lobbying by business interests: school districts were blocked from raising local taxes, and a statewide tax increase to aid schools was targeted for repeal.[141]

HOW MUCH IS TOO MUCH?

Concerns such as these help animate increasingly vocal opposition to school commercialism, yet the reaction is far from uniform. An editorial writer for the *Tampa Tribune* in Florida in 2003 approached the prospect of naming rights matter-of-factly. Noting that naming rights and school bus advertising are already a fact in other communities, the writer, William Yelverton, suggested that the Pasco, Florida, school district should follow suit. Dismissing concerns that such a move "sends a bad message, especially to youngsters—namely, that anything is for sale at the right price," Yelverton asserted it was merely a matter of being creative, "stepping outside the tradition [sic] box," and was preferable to "being forced to eliminate jobs, an entire department even."[142]

The editorial board at the *Arkansas Democrat-Gazette* in Little Rock disagreed, however. In a 2003 editorial about the decision of school officials in Harrison, Arkansas, to name their renovated football stadium for FedEx Freight in return for $1 million, the newspaper agonized. Corporate sponsors at the school, the editorial noted, adopt classrooms and "do things like provide classroom supplies and pay for special projects. Which sounds great. But in return, the kids spend time learning about the corporation. Which sounds less than great. Is the kids' time being traded for a corporate handout? Shouldn't class time be spent on more basic education—like math, science, English, and history? Just what message are we sending the kids when we make deals like these?"[143]

The editorial drew a distinction between naming rights for an individual benefactor and for a corporation, and likened the latter to "a commercial trade-off" akin to advertising. "Which is fine in its place, but its place shouldn't be in the public schools. Or on their football stadiums. Some things money shouldn't be able to buy."[144]

Proponents of increased business–school partnerships contend that corporate involvement in education benefits students. The National Association of Partners in Education—a business group founded to promote corporate–school relationships—claims that research shows "improved achievement ... [and] a reduction in 'risk behaviors' such as alcohol use and discipline problems" among students who are involved in "partnership activities" that involve businesses in the school.[145] The Harris Interactive/Kid Power Poll of Youth Marketers, conducted in February 2004, found that 74 percent of professionals who market to young people expect to see in-school marketing increase—driven by schools' tighter budgets and need for new funding sources.[146]

Even the youth marketers—who, by their professional association, might be expected to have a bias in favor of marketing activities in general—are clearly disquieted by the extent of marketing's reach into the schools. Among the 878 respondents in the online poll, substantial majorities approved of corporate sponsorship of sports events (84 percent), loyalty-based fund-raising programs like Box Tops for Education (83 percent), advertising in school papers (73 percent), and corporate logos on sports uniforms (65 percent). Yet these respondents were deeply divided on the question of how far is too far: While 45 percent said youths could handle in-school advertising, 47 percent said that schools should be off-limits.[147]

MARKETING AN IDEOLOGY OF CONSUMERISM

School commercialism serves three distinct functions. It provides corporations with a venue in which to market products and services. It also provides them with a podium from which to disseminate corporate ideas about topics important to their interests. Corporate-sponsored curriculum materials, for example, represent the self-interested point of view of the corporation or industry about controversial subjects such as the Exxon Valdez oil spill or environmental policy. Finally, school commercialism becomes a vehicle through which corporations can deliver a broader ideological message promoting consumption as the primary source of well-being and happiness.

Equating the good life with consumption is central to the ideology of marketing. Marketers teach that one should be perpetually dissatisfied, and that dissatisfaction can best be alleviated by consuming something. In essence, marketing seeks to replace humane values with mercantile ones. By equating "more" with "good," the culture of consumption teaches that more televisions, more toys, more clothes—more of everything an American can buy—results in more happiness. As David Riesman,[148] Vance Packard,[149] and more recently, Sut Jhally,[150] have argued, however, consumer values lead not to happiness, but to alienation, loneliness, and loss of freedom.

Uncovering and scrutinizing the influence of corporations in public schools ultimately forces us to grapple with the question of what our schools are for. The American ideal of public education has historically been conceived as a means for preparing the next generation to participate fully in a free and democratic society—a role that sometimes means challenging the status quo and established power structures. The more corporate special interests are allowed to influence what schools teach—and, by extension, limit what they cannot teach—the less students are seen as active citizens-to-be, and the more they are seen as passive consumers-to-be-sold.

3

EAT, DRINK, AND BE DIABETIC: USING SCHOOLS TO PROMOTE ILLNESS

In the fall of 1999, Fleming Elementary School in Detroit opened a McDonald's outlet to help students learn to read. As part of an elaborate incentive program, students who read specified books, took quizzes on them, and demonstrated good school attendance were able to earn the chance to buy meals at an in-school "Mini McDonald's." The food was shipped hot from a nearby McDonald's restaurant, and local college students painted a mural of the fast food chain's characters on the school cafeteria walls. Children could apply at the school's "employment office" to serve the meals. School display cases were stocked with McDonald's-related prizes.[1]

The program was short-lived; by September 2004, it was no longer in existence.[2] Although this program may have been ephemeral, what it represents is not. Over the last two decades, two American institutions — public schools and the food marketing industry — have established a large number of increasingly varied connections.

SELLING FAT, SALT, AND SUGAR

Some of the oldest examples of corporate-sponsored curricula involve foods, such as counting games for young children using Cheerios or M&M's. In the early 1990s, the Campbell Soup Co., the marketers of Prego spaghetti sauce, constructed what was purported to be a lesson in the scientific method, whereby students would compare the thickness of Prego and its rival, Ragu.[3] An example of blatant huckstering, the Prego example may nonetheless be comparatively innocuous from the standpoint of nutrition. Recent developments, though, are more disquieting. Schools welcome fast food purveyors that provide their products as academic incentives, and the schools, under exclusive contracts, sell commercially branded fast food products in their lunchrooms and soft drinks in their vending machines. Schools air print and television advertisements for fast foods, candy, and soft drinks, and they form partnerships with food marketers in fund-raising schemes.

From the Basic 4 Food Guide to the Food Pyramid Guide, from health class to physical education, America's parents have relied on their public schools to help teach their children about good health and nutrition. Increasingly, though, the food industry is putting its thumb on the scales of learning, and children's health is suffering as a consequence. Exclusive marketing arrangements with soft drink and fast food companies; vending machines offering candy and high-fat, salty snacks; "educational materials" sponsored by fast food outlets; incentive programs and contests that encourage the consumption of foods high in fat and sugar; and direct advertising of junk food on Channel One and via other electronic marketing media constitute a pervasive informal curriculum that sends children powerful and harmful health messages.

Schools are not simply passive marketing venues in this process. Consider, for example, an arrangement that Radford High School in Hawaii struck with Coca-Cola several years ago. The program, established in 1999, issued students a special school identification card that also functioned as a debit card for purchases at the school cafeteria, school store, and concession stands. The card tracked students' purchases and tallied loyalty points for each meal or Coca-Cola product bought at school. The points could then be traded in for discounts at local merchants.[4] In short, with the school's imprimatur, the program encouraged students to consume more Coke products and rewarded them materially for doing so.

This especially aggressive marketing campaign may stand out, but only by degree. Exclusive marketing agreements whereby soft drink manufacturers are guaranteed to be the only provider of beverages on school premises (except for milk in the school cafeteria) for a period of time, in return for providing the school or school district with a percentage of the revenue generated, are widespread. And they have remained so in the face of growing criticism.

AGREEMENTS GET RICHER

It's not hard to see why. In 2002, the county school district in Charleston, South Carolina, agreed to an $8.1 million, five-year contract with the Pepsi Bottling Group to change all school vending machines over to Pepsi products.[5] The contract included a $1 million signing payment, which the district applied to its 2001 budget to offset state funding cuts, and a $50,000 annual payment from Pepsi after that, plus a 40 to 43 percent cut of machine revenues. The marketers appear to know what it takes to sell such deals: In the Charleston contract,

Pepsi agreed to offer $1,000 scholarships in district high schools and to assist booster clubs with concession sales and fund-raising programs. The company also included incentives to drive up sales, such as free movie, concert, or sporting-event tickets, and offered schools that install more machines a slightly higher share of the profits.

It is not surprising that school districts facing increasingly strained budgets find the prospect of additional revenue attractive and sign on the dotted line. "I agree that sodas are not the best thing in the world for you, but we have to find every possible resource to educate our children," a school board member told the *St. Petersburg Times* about a $50 million, 10-year contract between Pepsi-Cola and the Hillsborough County School District in Florida. While noting further the school district's "obligation" to provide healthy food and teach about healthy diets, the board member, Candy Olson, added: "I don't think the schools have the responsibility of being the food police. And I don't think schools should be expected to turn up their noses" at $4 million annually.[6]

Money or not, exclusive agreements are contentious. Consider the reaction of an Edwardsville, Missouri, high school principal, Norm Bohnenstiehl, who told the *St. Louis Post-Dispatch* in 2003 that there "haven't been any drawbacks" to a Coca-Cola pouring rights contract, which paid for a new track, scoreboards, and auditorium improvements.[7] A Columbia, Missouri, parent and dietician, Melinda Hemmelgarn, expressed the counterview, arguing, "Schools should be commercial-free zones," while a high school student, noting the number of students who drank soda and chips in their first classes of the day, asserted, "Schools are pushing for students to adopt an unhealthy and addictive habit."[8]

Some school districts have a history of being only too anxious to cooperate with their soft drink marketing partners. In 1997, the Grapevine-Colleyville School District in the Dallas-Fort

Worth area signed a 10-year, $4 million exclusive agreement with Dr. Pepper, under which the district allowed the company to paint its logo atop the high school building — where it could be seen from planes taking off and landing at Dallas-Fort Worth International Airport.[9]

While soft drinks account for the vast majority of exclusive agreements, other foods are involved as well. In 2003, in Tarrant County, Texas, Carroll School District trustees signed deals putting Chick-fil-A and Little Caesars Pizza products on campuses and at stadium events, for $603,000 in sponsorship rights and sales profits for one year.[10]

LET THEM EAT PIZZA

Exclusive agreements are not the only means by which food marketers connect with schools. Incentive programs such as Pizza Hut's "Book-It" promotion, which awards individual size pizzas to students who reach certain reading goals, [11] offer industry another opening. There is a wide range of such programs. While Pizza Hut's is the most famous and probably the largest, rivals are also in on the act. For example, Papa John's Pizza outlets give schools "Winner's Circle" cards for free pizza, donuts, ice cream, video games, and museum visits, to be distributed to students who earn all Cs or better on report cards.[12]

Yet another link between schools and food marketers occurs in fund-raising programs that employ schoolchildren to sell candy, pizzas, and other products on behalf of local parent–teacher groups. The U.S. Centers for Disease Control and Prevention (CDC) reports that the most widespread fund-raising products sold in schools are candy and high-fat baked goods.[13] Such organizations typically contract with for-profit marketers, who in turn share a portion of the profits with the sponsoring schools. In essence, such agreements amount to school associations agreeing to allow children to sell products for for-profit companies in return for a cut of the proceeds.

Other food-related fund-raising programs are built around customer brand loyalty. Grocery stores such as Giant Eagle use customer loyalty cards as a vehicle for recording purchase amounts and awarding to designated schools a percentage of the customer's purchases.[14] Campbell's Labels for Education — founded in 1973—and General Mills' Box Tops for Education are the two mostly widely known rewards programs, and schools readily encourage parents and neighbors to purchase the companies' products so that the appropriate labels or box tops can be collected in order to be redeemed for rewards.[15] Tyson Foods and Community Coffee have similar programs.[16]

The General Mills program was expanded significantly by the 2002 merger of General Mills and Pillsbury, resulting in the expansion of Box Tops for Education. The program rewards schools for submitting coupons worth 10 cents each clipped from the company's products. The merger more than doubled the number of affiliated brands from 330 to 800; besides Cheerios and Wheaties, now consumers can collect fund-raising coupons from brands such as Pillsbury, Green Giant, Progresso, and Gold Medal Flour, to name just a few. As of 2002, the company reported that more than 71,000 schools participated and more then 22 million households were clipping the company's box tops and other coupons.[17] Campbell's Labels for Education, meanwhile, has over the course of 30 years traded $100 million in school supplies in return for labels collected by schools.[18] Tyson Foods, begun in 1999, gives schools up to 24 cents per label turned in, to a maximum of $12,000 a year.[19]

BILLIONS SERVED, PENNIES FOR SCHOOLS

McDonald's Corp. practices yet another form of fund-raising food marketing. Annually, the fast food chain puts teachers and principals in school districts around the country to work for an evening, donating some of their revenues for the evening back to schools.[20] A 2002 press release from the fast food chain boasted participation of 700 schools in 16 states for the "McTeacher's Night," generating $400,000. The number looks impressive until one does the math: In return for free publicity, not to mention making a favorable, brand-loyalty-building impression on participating teachers' students and their families, the program fetched on average less than $600 per school.[21]

In 1997, the Denver School District created a program called "Community Sponsorship of the Curriculum" and invited local and national companies to support the district's education programs in return for advertising rights throughout the district. Sunkist, for example, sponsored the Comprehensive Health Initiative. In return, the company was given space for its "Just One — A Whole Day's Vitamin C" advertising campaign on school buses, scoreboards, and print material sent home with students.[22]

In 2002, Safeway produce suppliers placed a promotional program in schools featuring 14 professional U.S. soccer stars as spokespeople to encourage children to eat five servings of fruits and vegetables a day. About 1,500 stores adopted local schools, gave tours of the produce section to students, and gave teachers packets that included a wall chart that students could use to track consumption of fruits and vegetables. "Kids who ate five servings each day scored a soccer player bookmark," and the company noted subsequently higher fruit and vegetable sales.[23] "It worked because the cause is bullet-proof," the consultant who handled the program bragged. "No one could [complain that] we were trying to sell kids more produce."[24]

But some do complain. "Why does nutrition education have to be linked to a corporation?" asked Susan Linn, a Harvard psychiatry instructor and founder of an advocacy group, Stop Commercial Exploitation of Children. "If we as a society believe nutrition is important for kids, why aren't we doing more to support those programs?"[25]

MARKETING JUJITSU

Marketers have been ingenious at subverting critiques of their actions. In 1997, Nabisco asserted in its advertising that every bag of its Chips Ahoy! cookies contained at least a thousand chips. Elementary school students in Wadesboro, North Carolina, challenged the company, and 130 of them wrote letters claiming they could find only 600 chips in a bag Accused of false advertising and lying to customers, Nabisco didn't shrink from the controversy; instead, it launched a contest — and got schools to cooperate. Students were asked to verify that there were indeed a thousand chips in every bag of Chips Ahoy! cookies. Contestants then sent in essays or videos that demonstrated ingenious ways of counting the chips. Three finalists competed for the top prize of $25,000 in scholarships. The result, noted the trade journal *Selling to Kids:* Nabisco not only got extensive press coverage, but the company also gained "access to schools and kids nationwide."[26]

Marketers often advertise to children by purporting to teach about advertising, such as a competition sponsored by the Mars candy company, which created a half-finished Halloween commercial for students to complete. The ad was broadcast in 1997 on Channel One News, the 12-minute current events program containing two minutes of commercials broadcast into approximately 12,000 middle and high schools. Students then got to vote on one of three endings. By casting their vote via a toll-free telephone call, students were entered in a sweepstakes with two $5,000 first prizes and 100 second prizes of 24 compact discs.[27]

Some promotional schemes dispense completely with any pedagogical overlay. In December 2001, Cadbury Schweppes, the world's fourth-largest confectioner according to *Advertising Age,* announced it would distribute 500,000 free book covers to middle school children, containing samples of its Sour Patch Kids and Swedish Fish candies.[28]

SCHOOL FINANCES DON'T IMPROVE; STUDENT HEALTH GETS WORSE

Corporate motivation for such programs is clear enough. Like every other form of advertising and promotion, they are designed to boost sales and profits. "The school system is where you build brand loyalty," said John Alm, president and chief operating officer of Coca-Cola Enterprises (a national bottling firm affiliated with the soft drink maker), in a remark reported by the *Atlanta Journal-Constitution* in 2003.[29]

Marketers repeatedly insist that these activities benefit schools. The typical exclusive contract with a soft drink bottler, for example, gives a school or district a percentage of the sales derived from soft drink purchases. In some cases, there are additional incentives such as scoreboards, coolers, and free products for special events.[30]

The conversion of our schools into advertising and marketing venues for the food industry, however — especially for those segments that produce the least healthful products — has wide-ranging negative consequences. To begin with, there is evidence that schools suffer financially from such arrangements. A 2003 study by the Texas state agricultural commissioner, Susan Combs, concluded that school vending machines cost schools' food services in the state $60 million in sales annually. Combs sought open records information on school district vending contracts, and reported that 52 percent of the districts that responded had exclusive food and drink vending contracts.[31]

A newspaper's examination in 2004 of the Charleston, South Carolina, agreement with Pepsi found that the schools' actual net from the agreement fell short of projections, with some school principals claiming their schools got back less money under the agreement than they had from past vending arrangements and demanding a contract renegotiation.[32]

If some exclusive agreements are fiscally questionable, they are all nutritionally suspect. Accompanying the growth of these marketing practices has been a significant and alarming rise in obesity among young people. In three decades, the average American's soda consumption has more than doubled — from 22.4 gallons in 1970 to 56.1 gallons in 1998, according to the Beverage Marketing Corp.[33] In a landmark 1998 study, the Center for Science in the Public Interest found that among teenage boys a quarter drank more than two 12-ounce cans per day, and that 5 percent drank more than five cans.[34]

More recent medical findings have found cause for even greater alarm. Girls, although they drink about a third less than boys, face potentially more serious health consequences. With soda displacing milk from their diets, an increasing number of girls may be candidates for osteoporosis. In 2000, Harvard researchers found that physically active girls who drink soda are three times as likely to suffer bone fractures as girls who never drink soda. If the soda of choice is cola, the risk increases five times.[35] With childhood obesity rates soaring, William Dietz, director of the Division of Nutrition at the U.S. Centers for Disease Control and Prevention (CDC), as far back as 1999 suggested, "If the schools must have vending machines, they should concentrate on healthy choices like bottled water."[36] Richard Troiano, a National Cancer Institute senior scientist, has said that the data suggest a possible link between childhood obesity and soda consumption, with overweight children taking in more calories from soda than their nonover-weight peers.[37]

OBESITY: A MARKER FOR ILL HEALTH

Obesity is both a problem in itself and a more general indicator of the health of children. As such, it has been the subject of considerable recent research and it has become a growing concern among policymakers. The CDC has reported that obesity in children has tripled in the last two decades. Citing 1999–2000 data, the CDC reported in October 2002 that 15 percent of children and teenagers (9 million) aged 6 to 19 were overweight, with a body mass index at or about the 95th percentile.[38] The CDC report came on the heels of an October 2002 White House-sponsored conference "Healthy Schools." Speakers lamented rising malnourishment as well as obesity among children, while health classes are eliminated and vending machines and less-than-healthful cafeteria menus continue to influence students' nutritional choices.[39] RAND Corporation researchers reported in 2002 that obesity is "linked to a big increase in chronic health conditions and significantly higher health expenditures. And it affects more people than smoking, heavy drinking, or poverty."[40] A study reported in the *Journal of the American Medical Association* in August 2004 found that among women, drinking more sugar- or corn-syrup-sweetened soft drinks increases their risk of developing type II diabetes and of gaining weight.[41] Meanwhile, even as schools are participating in programs that encourage more consumption of unhealthful food products, they are cutting back on much-needed physical education programs that might offset the sedentary lives of so many children. A September 2004 study from the National Institute of Medicine found that more than 90 percent of elementary schools, middle schools, and high schools offer physical education classes less frequently than the thirty minutes to one hour a day recommended by the institute.[42] Perhaps this explains why fast food and soft drink marketers are countering criticism by promoting exercise. McDonald's, for instance, has retooled its Ronald McDonald mascot as a "health ambassador," offering to send him around to schools to promote fitness.[43]

DIVIDED LOYALTIES

In the face of such alarming health trends, exclusive agreements — indeed, any arrangements that use schools to market unhealthful foods and beverages — put schools squarely on the wrong side of the issue. To fully understand the implications of such arrangements, think back to the agreement between Coca-Cola and Colorado Springs District 11, discussed in Chapter 2. At the time of signing, the district projected that the 10-year exclusive agreement would be worth about $8.1 million, a figure that represented less than 1 percent of the district's budget. The terms of the agreement, however, raised the contract's worth to $11.1 million if the district met "sales incentive thresholds."[44] The existence of "sales incentives" underlines the kind of conflict of interest inherent in exclusive sales agreements: The agreement did not merely call for the Colorado Springs School District to profit from the sale of a particular brand of soft drink. It was also a financial incentive to promote the greatest possible consumption of that soft drink — in short, placing the district in the position of implicitly asking students to ignore the health and nutrition advice they get from classroom curriculum. The North Carolina School Nutrition Action Committee (SNAC) (a joint project of the state's Department of Public Instruction, Department of Health and Human Services, and Cooperative Extension Service) warns that contracts linking school payments to consumption are particularly harmful to children's health.[45]

Rather than promoting healthy choices, exclusive agreements put pressure on school districts to increase the number of soft drink vending machines in schools in order to increase sales. Daniel Michaud, business administrator for the Edison, New Jersey, public schools, told the *Washington Post* in 1999 that before signing an exclusive contract with Coke, few Edison schools had vending machines. After signing the contract, most district high schools had four machines, middle schools had three, and elementary schools had one.[46] As Kelly Mullen, a student at a Rhode Island high school with an exclusive contract, commented, "There's really nothing else to drink."[47] That's exactly the way the bottlers that seek exclusive agreements want it. Christine Smith, director of community partnerships and enterprise activity for the Denver Public Schools, put it to the *Denver Business Journal* this way: "Exclusivity made the difference. The question was, 'How much is it worth to get rid of the competition?' The answer was, 'Quite a lot.'"[48]

A 2000 report from the U.S. General Accounting Office underscored the fact that schools found product sales — mainly soft drinks — to be the single most lucrative source of outside revenue.[49] A follow-up report in 2004 from the agency (now renamed the U.S. Government Accountability Office) elaborated. The report, *School Meal Programs: Competitive Foods Are Available in Many Schools*, helps explain why schools stand by arrangements that potentially harm their students. In a study of school a la carte offerings, the GAO found that while many schools offered healthful fruits, vegetables, and juices, financial problems compromised those efforts. "School food authority officials told us that financial pressures have led them to serve less healthful a la carte items because these items generate needed revenue," said the GAO report.[50] The report also noted that soft drinks, ice cream, and salty, high-fat snacks were the items students purchased most often from vending machines.[51]

The result is that school districts often resist giving up the contracts, fearing that the loss of funds will further hamper their operations, and sometimes join campaigns to turn back bans on soda in schools. "Simply banning soft drinks will have little impact on the problem" of obesity, the executive director of the National Association of State Boards of Education complained in a letter to the editor of *Education Week* in the fall of 2003, adding later, "We also should not ignore the unintended consequences of restricting schools' freedom to create business partnerships at a time when cuts in school budgets make every dollar count."[52]

INTERNAL CONTRADICTIONS

A study in the *Journal of School Health* published in February 2004 zeroed in on the internal contradictions in the thinking of school board members. On the one hand, board members responding to an attitude survey spoke in support of "providing healthy food options, establishing minimum nutrition standards for fast foods, and limiting and monitoring food and soda advertisements in their districts."[53] On the other hand, however, "of those who knew they had an exclusive beverage vendor contract, just 31 percent did not agree with awarding such a contract, and 26 percent wholly supported it," the researchers wrote. "Thus, many board members remain uncommitted on this issue, presumably either from lack of familiarity with the issue, or lack of priority where it is concerned."[54]

Individual states and the federal government have laws and regulations that are supposed to reduce student consumption of less healthful foods on school grounds. For example, the U.S. Department of Agriculture (USDA) classifies soft drinks as a "food of minimal nutritional value" and prohibits their sale during lunch periods. The USDA has issued model regulations aimed at elementary schools that would ban soft drinks (and other nonnutritious foods) from school grounds entirely from the start of classes until the end of the lunch period. Secondary schools, the agency has pointed out, have the authority to completely ban the sale of foods of minimal nutritional value.[55] Guidelines similar to those proposed by the USDA have been adopted in Kentucky and Florida.[56] Other states have similar laws. In Texas in 2003, the Department of Agriculture called on elementary schools to "prevent students from accessing FMNVs [Foods of minimal nutritional value] on school premises. Such food and beverages may not be sold or given away on school premises . . . during the school day."[57]

Yet in West Virginia, for example, a 2004 study by the state Education Department's Office of Child Nutrition found that a state law requiring soda and snack machines to be turned off during breakfast and lunch periods was seldom enforced. The report recommended that the state school board require counties, not schools, to approve and sign beverage contracts and review them to prohibit aggressive marketing. The report also recommended that more healthful alternatives to soft drinks, such as milk, juice, and water, be made available at competitive prices.[58] On the heels of the report, an (unsuccessful) candidate for governor in the state vowed to remove junk food from schools if he were elected.[59]

Corporate arrangements not only undermine nutrition lessons; they can undermine other educational priorities as well. That was the ultimate message of what happened to 15-year-old Andrea Boyes in 2002. Andrea, a student at West Salem High School in Oregon, wanted to raise money for the cheerleading squad to which she belonged. Andrea devised a plan to resell bottled water at a dollar a bottle, and managed a deal that allowed the squad to net 55 cents of that. She designed her own label featuring the school's logo for the fund-raiser bottles,[60] and she hoped to harvest enough profits to create a scholarship program that would allow teenagers at her school who could not afford the cost of cheerleading uniforms or tryouts to be able to join the squad.[61]

Instead of winning praise from principals, teachers, or the PTA, she hit a roadblock. A Pepsi-Cola exclusive contract at West Salem High School where Andrea Boyes was enrolled barred her from selling the water on school grounds.[62] For Gary Boyes, Andrea's father, the incident was a wake-up call that raised questions about "the actual rights of the contracting parties to inhibit student rights and modify accepted uses of publicly owned properties."[63]

Programs to market food products and beverages in schools in return for some form of payback to the schools undermine curricula and potentially undermine student health. Because they are so pervasive, they also can act as a sort of conceptual gateway, opening schools up to other forms of commercial involvement. A *Tampa Tribune* editorial writer, advocating in 2003 that the cash-strapped Pasco, Florida, school district sell naming rights and advertising on buses, observed in support of his proposal, "The district already has a contract with Pepsi for exclusive beverage rights in schools. The door has already been open.[sic]"[64] At the same time, however, marketing unhealthful foods in schools is becoming a point of contention. In the same community, an editorial writer for the competing *St. Petersburg Times* penned a commentary lauding two Pasco County schools for rejecting Pepsi contracts for vending machines that would have operated all day.[65] The differing editorial views illustrate how marketing unhealthful foods in schools is becoming a point of dispute in some communities.

CITIZENS REACT, GOVERNMENT FOLLOWS

There are signs of a growing backlash against school commercialism in general, and commercialism that is perceived as a threat to children's health in particular. The $8.1 million agreement between Charleston, South Carolina, schools and Pepsi in 2002 mentioned earlier led one parent to complain that it "puts people in the unfortunate position of encouraging students to drink soda so the school can fund things."[66] Citing the soda-linked problems of obesity, childhood diabetes, and weak bones, the parent, nurse Kate Young, added, "We really recognize that the district is under enormous financial strain. . . . But do we want [students'] health to be what is used to make up for the budget shortfall?"[67] While parents subsequently considered challenging the agreement,[68] that appears not to have gotten anywhere.[69]

In Norfolk, Virginia, similar health objections were raised to a 2002 agreement to sell only Coca-Cola products under a $3.2 million contract over five years.[70] As Pepsi did in Charleston, Coke agreed to pay Norfolk schools more if they sold more of the drink's 20-ounce bottles.[71]

School districts, teachers, parents, and policymakers have begun to look critically at corporate marketing and its impact on children's health. For example, PTAs and citizens groups such as Obligation (Alabama), the Citizen's Campaign for Commercial-Free Schools (Seattle), and Parents Advocating School Accountability (San Francisco) have spoken out against school commercialism. Local school boards have also taken action. In Seattle, advertising was severely restricted, and in Los Angeles, the school board has banned the sale of soft drinks beginning in 2004, citing an epidemic of adolescent obesity in its decision. In San Francisco, Aptos Middle School tested the effect of banning junk food in January 2003.[72] The school's action was the precursor to what has since become a districtwide ban.

In Seattle, Washington, the school board in 2003 agreed to limits on an exclusive agreement with Coca-Cola, but stopped short of an outright ban on soft drink sales[73] in a deal worth about $390,000 a year.[74] The board required Coke to reserve three slots in each vending machine for water and 100 percent fruit juice, added a clause allowing it to cancel the new five-year agreement, and required that middle school vending machines be turned off until after school each day.[75] While threats of a lawsuit[76] did not appear to deter the district, the board revisited the issue in 2004 and toughened up its rules — implementing much stronger policies against commercialism, including a ban on soft drink and junk food sales.[77]

GUIDELINES AND LAWS

A number of professional organizations have developed voluntary guidelines to help determine which, if any, corporate-sponsored materials have merit. These organizations include the National Education Association, the Society of Consumer Affairs Professionals in Business, and the various organizations that have adopted the Milwaukee Principles for Corporate Involvement in the Schools.[78] The National Association of State Boards of Education has developed sample policies to promote healthy eating,[79] and the American Academy of Pediatrics has taken positions critical of advertising aimed at children and of school-based advertising that promotes unhealthy lifestyle choices in particular.[80] The American Academy of Pediatrics in January 2004 issued a statement declaring that soft drinks don't belong in schools and calling for pediatricians to take up the fight to remove them.[81] The National Institute of Medicine, meanwhile, released a report in the fall of 2004 calling for an end to advertising in schools.[82] The issue has become an international concern: In 2004, the World Health Organization found that "only a handful" of nations have any regulations applying to the sales of certain food products in schools, and made the case for stricter regulation worldwide.[83]

Local and statewide bans on soft drink sales in schools have begun to take hold. In Lake County, Florida, near Orlando, the school board voted in December 2003 to limit vending machine sales to water, juice, and sports drinks — and gave up a $5 million, 10-year contract with Pepsi as well; members cited nutritional concerns.[84] Meanwhile, though, in the Hillsborough District — site of the $50-million deal — Principal Tom Rao dismissed as "a reactionary thing" a state bill to ban carbonated and high-sugar drinks from school vending machines.[85]

Nevertheless, in recent years, some momentum has built for bans. Philadelphia public schools banned selling soda in an action initiated in 2003 by Schools Chief Executive Paul G. Vallas, unhappy because of poor nutrition and increasing childhood obesity.[86] The district followed through in early 2004, with the School Reform Commission voting 3 to 2 to permit only 100 percent juice drinks; drinking water without sweeteners, flavors, or colors; and milk and milk-flavored drinks.[87] In doing so, the district was following a trend evident throughout suburban Philadelphia's school districts.[88] In Chicago Public Schools, CEO Arne Duncan banned soda and junk foods from vending machines in the spring of 2004[89] after aldermen the previous fall sought limits on "the sale of minimally nutritious food and beverages."[90] The Austin, Texas, school district approved a districtwide ban on sodas and junk food in vending machines in 2003, although under USDA rules, chocolate bars, chips, and sugar-laden pastries were still permitted, along with more healthful snacks such as canned tuna, trail mix, and baked potato chips.[91] In 2004, the DeKalb County (Georgia) School Board barred schools from selling soft drinks, candy, and other items during the school day.[92]

State legislators have begun to act as well. Under the Competitive Foods Policy of North Carolina, implemented in 2003, schools were ordered not to sell "competitive foods" — that is, foods competing with lunchroom offerings — in or within 35 feet of school lunchrooms, unless profits funded school lunch programs. Only high schools were permitted to sell sodas, but not during lunch periods, and foods of minimal nutritional value were barred from a la carte lines.[93] In September 2003, California's then-Governor Gray Davis signed the "California Childhood Obesity Prevention Act" (SB 677).[94] The act restricted junk food and candy sales in schools.[95] It limited elementary schools to selling water, milk, or 100 percent fruit juice, and middle schools to selling water, milk, fruit drinks with at least 50 percent juice and no added sugar, and sports drinks such as Gatorade.[96]

REGULATION'S MIXED RESULTS

Not all such statewide attempts have succeeded. A review of legislative activity between 1999 and 2003 by the Commercialism in Education Research Unit found 30 pieces of legislation and 3 resolutions that specifically addressed health-related schoolhouse commercialism issues at the federal and state level. Of the 30 pieces, 17 failed, 5 passed, and 8 were pending as of July 2003.[97] Of the 3 resolutions introduced, 2 failed and 1 passed. And in 2004 alone, as many as 15 states introduced legislation restricting school vending machine sales.[98]

On the other hand, in some states, the trend was reversed. Florida, for example, had issued guidelines barring the sale of soda in schools until one hour after the last lunch period of the day. In 2003, the state changed its rules to permit soda sales all day if noncarbonated fruit juices were also available.[99] The development points at another wrinkle in the debate over exclusive agreements and student health. Not infrequently, one proffered solution is, instead of removing unhealthful products such as sugary sodas, to expand the offerings of more healthful ones, such as fruit juices, water, or milk. Bringing in more healthful products sounds for the most part like a positive development. At times, however, more healthful options appear to give school districts political cover for not rejecting less healthful ones.

In Georgia, for example, the Cherokee County School Board in 2004 rejected a plan that would have limited the sale of soft drinks by permitting them only in the gymnasium or cafeteria areas. In deciding not to change its current policy, which permitted sweet drinks and fatty foods, the district's superintendent, Frank Petruzielo, said the board reasoned it was enough that vending machines already offered more nutritious products such as low-fat pretzels, fruit leather snacks, and trail mix.[100]

South Carolina's state Senate Education Committee in 2003 took up a bill that would bar junk food from schools that didn't comply with dietary requirements of the National School Lunch Act. The legislation would eliminate vending machines, fast food, and candy sales of nonnutritious foods high in calories, fat, or sugar, and would permit the sale on school premises only of 100 percent fruit juices and water, low-fat milk, and other more nutritious offerings.[101] As of late 2004, however, it had yet to gain passage.

In addition to sparking criticism from health authorities, exclusive drink contracts from time to time draw opposition from competing businesses. A Syracuse, New York-based maker of sports drinks, American Quality Beverages (AQB), in 2003 sued the Fulton, New York, school district, alleging that its ten-year, $500,000 contract with Coke circumvented a competitive bidding process that the firm had won to sell Z'Lektra sports drinks in area schools; the agreement was voided as a result of the Coke deal.[102] New York's Commissioner of Education, Richard P. Mills, issued a statement in March 2004 reiterating the importance of competitive bidding under New York's education laws.[103] (The AQB lawsuit remains pending.[104]) Meanwhile, in 2003 Gary Boyes, fresh from his battle on behalf of his daughter Andrea, sued his Oregon school district for requiring his children to watch Channel One. The lawsuit, still pending as of late 2004, alleges that the district's contract with the broadcaster amounted to an unlawful delegation of powers to educate schoolchildren reserved to the government under the Oregon Constitution.[105] Meanwhile, George Washington University law professor John Banzhaf III has joined the issue, proposing lawsuits similar to the tobacco litigation against school districts that sign exclusive agreements with junk food and soft drink purveyors.[106]

THE FOOD INDUSTRY RETRENCHES

The food and beverage industries aren't ignoring the new pressure; indeed, they have undertaken a variety of projects aimed at countering a public relations backlash and, in all likelihood, at undermining possible legal restrictions on its advertising and marketing practices. Food manufacturers have adjusted their menus to be more healthful: Wendy's now offers orange slices instead of fries in its children's meals, and Oscar Mayer has added applesauce to its Lunchables, a product line of cheese, meats, and crackers packaged for easy snacking. Frito-Lay has introduced low-fat Doritos for sale in school lunchrooms.[107] An executive at PepsiCo told the *New York Times*, "The food business can play a very constructive role" in making more healthful foods "available to kids and marketing them in ways that make a healthier lifestyle more attractive."[108]

In 2003, Coke and its bottlers—"fighting to keep their presence in schools, amid criticism that soft drinks contribute to obesity among young people," in the words of the *Atlanta Journal-Constitution*[109]—brought out new "model guidelines" that ended the use of the soft drink maker's logos on textbooks and curriculum materials.[110] Coke also vowed to provide water, juices, and other drinks along with sodas where it sold soft drinks in schools.[111] Centerville, Ohio, pediatrician and school board member David Roer, whose school district has banned all soft drinks and replaced them in vending machines with water, milk, and juice, responded that the guidelines were "a good start from Coke, but the ultimate goal would be to get rid of carbonated beverages and provide more nutritious products."[112]

Of course, that is exactly what the industry does not want to do. Instead, Coca-Cola, for instance, has begun sponsoring after-school fitness programs, while PepsiCo has promised to pay $2 million a year for three years to deliver an in-school curriculum for health and science classes, Balance First, which seeks to encourage students to eat a hundred fewer calories a day and walk off daily an additional hundred calories.[113] As Banzhaf has pointed out, however, such campaigns are disingenuous. To burn the 800 calories in a McDonald's "Mighty Kids Meal," for instance, Banzhaf notes, " a typical 7-year old girl would have to walk for 9.3 hours, OR play volleyball for 8.1 hours, OR play baseball for 6.6 hours, OR swim or play paddleball for 5.4 hours, OR engage in aerobics for 5 hours."[114] A 10-year-old boy consuming a Big Mac, large fries, and McFlurry drink — not at all an unusual menu for such a child — would have to "walk for 15 hours, OR play volleyball for 13 hours, OR play baseball for 10.5 hours, OR swim or play paddleball for 8.8 hours, OR engage in aerobics for 8 hours" to burn off the meal's 1,790 calories.[115] Exercise has its place in fitness, Banzhaf concludes. But, he adds, "Telling kids that they can remain slim simply by engaging in regular exercise, and not passing up the Golden Arches, is deceptive, and teachers and schools should not cooperate."[116]

The industry's counterattack is multipronged. Even as it attempts to portray itself as a responsible force, it also seeks to dismiss evidence of the harm its products are causing. Thus, even as Coke was introducing its new guidelines in 2003, the soft drink industry also began circulating claims that the average middle- and high-school student consumed on average only one 16-ounce soda per week at school.[117] Soft drink marketers also formed a lobbying group to combat soda bans, the Center for Consumer Freedom[118]—an Orwellian title, given the fact that exclusive agreements deprive consumers the freedom to choose what they might buy.

The industry is also using concern about obesity to its advantage, while not giving an inch on the underlying issue of in-school marketing. PepsiCo attributed 56 percent of the growth in its North American revenue in the first half of 2004 to "healthful" products, including Quaker Oats cereals, Gatorade, Aquafina bottled waters, and baked and reduced-fat Frito-Lay snacks, and is branding such products with a green logo. The company has introduced 30 reduced-calorie drinks sold in schools and put 17,000 Aquafina and Gatorade machines in schools in 2003. Yet it continues to negotiate exclusive vending contracts with schools, and gives no indication of plans to halt the practice.[119]

FROM MARKETING ILLNESS TO MARKETING HEALTH

Throughout, the industry has sought to influence the terms, content, and tenor of the debate. "Blaming industry is not going to get us any closer to a solution," Richard Martin, a spokesman for the Grocery Manufacturers of America, told the *New York Times.* "The only way to get there is to work collaboratively, not by pointing fingers."[120]

Despite increased opposition, commercialism in schools is so pervasive that it remains difficult for many people to see. It blends seamlessly with the marketing maelstrom that defines contemporary American culture. Yet the evidence suggests that parents and ordinary citizens are much more concerned about the corporate exploitation of children in school than the professional educators to whom those children are entrusted.[121]

New York University professor of nutrition Marion Nestle has written extensively about the political power of the U.S. food industry and its impact on the health of Americans.[122] She predicts that it is unlikely that the federal government will ever undertake a comprehensive campaign to prevent obesity. In light of that, she asserts, it will take increased community opposition to avoid government agencies, including education agencies, from caving in to the "overwhelming industry pressures to eat more."[123]

For the foreseeable future, schools can be expected to remain an important food and beverage industry marketing battleground. Nearly a decade ago, G. David Van Houten, Jr., Coca-Cola Enterprises senior vice president and president of Coca-Cola Enterprises Central North American Group, laid down the gauntlet: "Schools — the education channel, youthful consumers — are important to everyone, and it has recently become a high-stakes game for that very reason. How much is that [school] business worth? I doubt we'll ever be able to answer that question fully. But we're going to continue to be very aggressive and proactive in getting our share of the school business."[124]

When marketers declare their goals, they must be taken seriously. This is one goal that, if achieved, will come at the expense of the health of our children.

4

CONTROLLING THE MASSES VS. LIBERATING THEM: EDWARD BERNAYS AND JOHN DEWEY CONSIDERED

The advertising industry is very effective at promoting the consumption of goods and services. At its heart, however, it is profoundly antidemocratic. A brief review of the historical development of modern marketing, the tools deployed by marketers to promote their client's interests when contrasted with the ideas of education philosopher John Dewey, illustrates the nature of the threat that modern mass marketing poses to democratic political institutions in general and public education in particular.

On April 20, 1914, in Ludlow, Colorado, the state militia opened fire on a tent city of striking miners and their families. Fifty-three people, including thirteen women and children, were killed in the massacre. The events in "bloody Ludlow" aroused widespread public sympathy for the Colorado Fuel and Iron Company strikers and provoked outrage at the mine owners, the Rockefeller family.

In response to inflamed public opinion, the Rockefellers hired Ivy Ledbetter Lee, a former newspaper reporter, to change the public perception of their mining operation and their family. To sell the corporate story and discredit the strikers, Lee oversaw the production of so-called fact sheets, recruited prominent people to write widely circulated letters in support of the mine owners, and heavily publicized John D. Rockefeller, Jr.'s trips to the Colorado mine site.

Mr. Lee's efforts, to a large extent, succeeded in quelling public hostility toward the mining company. Mr. Lee was, no doubt, well paid for his services, but we can be fairly certain that whatever he was paid, his public relations services cost a good deal less than it would have cost Rockefeller to raise wages, reduce the hours worked, or improve safety in the mines.[1]

THE BIRTH OF PUBLIC RELATIONS

Using his experience in the wake of the Ludlow bloodbath, Ivy Lee helped create the modern public relations industry. After his success in cleaning the stain of the Ludlow massacre off the Rockefeller image, Lee was kept on the family payroll to transform the public view of John D. Rockefeller, Sr. In the early years of the twentieth century, Rockefeller Sr.'s predatory business practices earned him a reputation as a callous villain. Wisconsin progressive Robert LaFollette, for example, called him "the greatest criminal of the age." To transform the public's opinion of Mr. Rockefeller, Lee saw to it that Rockefeller's philanthropy was prominently showcased and that newsreel footage showed him in appealing settings, such as handing out Christmas presents, joking with newsmen, singing with his family, and playing golf. By the time of John D. Rockefeller, Sr.'s death in 1937, his transformation from villain to civic benefactor in the public view was virtually complete. Lee had without question mastered the art of what he called "getting believed." [2]

A keen awareness of the importance in a democratic society of "getting believed" animated the work of Edward Bernays. Bernays was a nephew of Sigmund Freud through both of his parents: his mother was Sigmund Freud's sister, and his father was the brother of Freud's wife. He applied the science and art of psychology in a matter somewhat different from that of his famous and pioneering uncle, however. Bernays sought to harness social science research to the task he called "the engineering of consent." During World War I, he worked for the Committee on Public Information, helping the committee sell the Wilson administration's war policies. After the war, Bernays signed on as "public relations counsel" to an impressive list of America's most powerful corporations. The American Tobacco Company, for example, hired him to increase cigarette smoking among women. The tobacco industry was experiencing flat growth in demand for its product at a time when a huge number of potential smokers, woman, were stigmatized for smoking. The problem, from a marketing perspective, was how to remove the stigma. Bernays hit upon the idea of persuading New York socialites to march down Fifth Avenue in the 1929 New York City Easter Parade, proudly smoking cigarettes characterized as "torches of liberty" as a protest against women's inequality.[3]

In his career as a private "public relations counsel," and in a series of books such as *Crystallizing Public Opinion*,[4] *Propaganda*,[5] *The Engineering of Consent*,[6] and *Biography of an Idea: Memoirs of Public Relations Counsel*,[7] Bernays preached the gospel that public relations was essential in a democracy, and that social science knowledge was essential to public relations.

Bernays articulated his views quite clearly in his 1928 book *Propaganda*.[8] He begins the book by arguing, "The conscious and intelligent manipulation of the organized habits and opinions of the masses is an important element in democratic society. Those who manipulate this unseen mechanism of society constitute an invisible government which is the true ruling power of our country."[9] He continues:

> In theory, everybody buys the best and cheapest commodities offered him on the market. In practice, if everyone went around pricing, and chemically testing before purchasing, the dozens of soaps or fabrics or brands of bread which are for sale, economic life would become hopelessly jammed. To avoid such confusion, society consents to have its choice narrowed to ideas and objects brought to its attention by propaganda of all kinds. There is, consequently, a vast and continuous effort going on to capture our minds in the interest of some policy or commodity or idea.[10]

In Bernays' view, democratic civic life was a marketplace every bit as much as economic life. He took it as axiomatic that competing political interests would seek to put their views before the public just as competing economic interests would seek to promote their products and services. Bernays did not consider this an evil process, nor did he regard propaganda as a dirty word. To him, propaganda was "a perfectly legitimate form of human activity."[11] He argued, "Any society, whether it be social, religious, or political, which is possessed of certain beliefs, and sets out to make them known, either by the spoken or written words, is practicing propaganda."[12] Propaganda was, as he saw it, essential to keeping the wheels of politics and commerce turning while preserving social stability.

PR REPLACES THE ARISTOCRACY

The issue of how to have a democracy and at the same time restrain the mob and maintain social stability has occupied

American political theorists throughout history. In his historical analysis, Bernays expounded the view that "economic power tends to draw after it political power ... [and that] the industrial revolution shows how that power passed from the king and the aristocracy to the bourgeoisie."[13]

> Universal suffrage and *universal schooling* [emphasis added] reinforced this tendency, and at last even the bourgeoisie stood in fear of the common people. For the masses promised to become king. Today, however, a reaction has set in. The minority has discovered a powerful help in influencing majorities. It has been found possible so to mold the mind of the masses that they will throw their newly gained strength in the desired direction.[14]

Bernays argued that public relations and advertising are progressive tools of democratic governance and the market economy. His conflation of market choice and the democratic political process is, however, problematic for a number of reasons. By the end of the nineteenth century, American business and industry was, for the first time, able to produce more than Americans could consume. This did not mean that poverty had been abolished. It meant that more goods and services were available than Americans (given the social and economic structure of the time) could purchase. The problem facing the American economic system was in large measure how to promote and make possible mass consumption without threatening the position of the existing political and economic elites.

As Stuart Ewen writes in *Captains of Consciousness,* "It became a central function of business to be able to define a social order which would feed and adhere to the demands of the productive process and at the same time absorb, neutralize, and contain the transitional impulses of a working class emerging from the unrequited drudgery of nineteenth century industrialization."[15] Education was central to this process. It was, however, education of a very particular sort. Ewen quotes the Boston department store merchant, Edward

Filene, to make the point. Filene argued that "mass production demands the education of the masses,"[16] and that, in their education, "the masses must learn to behave like human beings in a mass production world."[17] According to Ewen, Filene wanted to build an industrial and social democracy based on what he termed "fact finding." To Filene, this meant that modern education should focus on "the 'facts' about what is being produced rather than questioning the social bases upon which those facts lay."[18]

The essentially conservative character of Filene's conception of education in an industrial democracy is suggested in Otis Pease's study of the development of American advertising between 1920 and 1940.[19] In discussing the consumer movement's response to advertising, Pease maintains that

> while the consumer movement was forced to attack advertising on the issue of its literal truthfulness, the advertising industry itself recognized that the question of literal truth or falsity was largely irrelevant, since the appeal of the advertisement lay not in the factual assertions of its contents but in the associations which it set up in the mind of the reader. This psychological factor to a great extent shifted the battle to a field where . . . the barrier between literal truth and literal falsity was obscured and where, in consequence, it lost much of its effectiveness. . . . The practices of the advertising men merely confirmed the suspicion that there existed in the industry no operating concept which would encourage the public to exercise free or rational judgments as consumers.[20]

One might add to Pease's comments the observation that a powerful, privately controlled institution that systematically sets out to undermine the ability of people to make rational judgments is inherently antidemocratic because it subverts the intellectual qualities and debases the civic relationships that make democratic life imaginable. What is, therefore, promoted to the detriment of genuine democratic civic culture is mass consumerism in commerce and politics.

ADVERTISING: TYING THE WATCHER TO THE SELLER

As Stuart and Elizabeth Ewen argue in *Channels of Desire,* published during the military buildup of the Reagan administration's early years, "The goal of the advertising industry is to link the isolated experience of the spectator with the collectivized impulses and priorities of the corporation.... If economic consumerism tends to organize disconnected individuals into coherent and predictable markets, it is political consumerism that defines the current state of western democracy seeking to create a vast patriotic unity ... a unity without solidarity."[21]

In other words, it is a unity defined by consumption rather than creation and participation.

In the false or virtual unity of consumer culture, the individual is thus more of a marketing icon than a social reality. Drawing on the work of Elizabeth Hurlock, the Ewens argue that although market research techniques "may be seen as ways of trying to understand how to 'paralyze the critical powers of an individual with the result that he or she follows the lead, whatever that lead may be,' fashion merchandisers attempted to surround the actual sales process with an aura of individuality."[22] For the Ewens, the individual in contemporary American society lives "in a visual space consumed by the imagery of commerce, a society organized around the purchase.... The 'constant rapidity' with which we are encouraged to tire of consumable objects, of our elusive pleasures, is generalized as an axiom for existence. To buy is to succeed."[23]

What this cultural value might portend for democratic institutions was described by an advertising executive writing anonymously in *The Nation* more than a half century ago: "Social scientists in the past have paid attention to the irrational patterns of human behavior because they wish to locate their social origins and thus be able to suggest changes that would result in more rational conduct. They now study irrationality ... and other aspects of human behavior ... to gather data that may be used by salesmen to manipulate consumers."[24] One outcome is no doubt the creation of what David Riesman termed the "lonely crowd"—a crowd that represents the negation of both the individual and genuine community.[25] Members of Riesman's lonely crowd define themselves by their possessions and express their individuality by looking, smelling, and thinking like everyone else.

THE VALUES OF MARKETING AND THE VALUES OF EDUCATION

As Ivy Leadbetter Lee and Edward Bernays were inventing the American public relations industry in the early twentieth century, John Dewey's ideas were challenging the received wisdom about the nature of the educational process. John Dewey's ideas were firmly rooted in American pragmatic philosophy and democratic social theory. For Dewey, an engaged democratic community built on rational interactions was necessary for the progressive development of humankind. Schools were, in his view, laboratories of democracy in which students learned democratic habits of cooperation and public service by living them in the classroom. Moreover, Dewey argued for a pedagogy guided by rational thought and problem-solving practice through which individuals could develop to their greatest capacity and contribute most effectively to democratic civic culture.

In every aspect, advertising ideology is the enemy of Dewey's philosophy. There is no place in the social theory that Bernays advanced and practiced, or in the work of his public relations offspring, for either Dewey's conception of democracy or his conception of an educative experience. Indeed, the edifice of American mass marketing is built on what, in *Experience and Education,* Dewey termed "mis-educative" experiences.

Sophisticated marketing techniques conceal but cannot alter the reality that the purpose of mass marketing is to manipulate the many for the benefit of the few. Marketing is, then, as Dewey characterized traditional education, imposition from above and from the outside.[26]

Today, the curriculum of our culture, 24 hours a day, 7 days a week, 365 days a year, is advertising. Advertising is omnipresent, saturating every public space. It has arguably superceded journalism as our culture's primary means of communication, squeezing out, marginalizing, and masquerading as virtually every other form of discourse. Every decision we make—from what to buy to whom we vote for—is, with few exceptions, shaped and influenced by messages bought and paid for by those who would profit from our decision. This is perhaps no more clearly seen than in our political campaigns, which are decided not on the basis of our careful reading of position papers or even of media reports on the candidates, but instead on the basis of carefully crafted 30- and 60-second television and radio spots that present highly emotional appeals and self-serving accounts of candidates, their policies, and their records.

As the curriculum of our daily life, advertising relentlessly miseducates Americans young and old every day—rendering our society correspondingly less democratic. In *Experience and Education,* Dewey wrote, "Any experience is miseducative that has the effect of arresting or distorting the growth of further experience. An experience may be such as to engender callousness; it may produce lack of sensitivity and of responsiveness. Then the possibilities of having richer experience in the future are restricted."[27]

He goes on to explain that miseducative experiences can land a person in a rut and limit further experience. Moreover, although miseducative experiences may be pleasurable or exciting in the moment, because they are not linked cumulatively, they simply dissipate energy. Miseducative experiences, according to Dewey, "may be lively, vivid, and 'interesting,' and yet their disconnectedness may artificially generate dispersive, disintegrated, centrifugal habits. The consequence of formation of such habits is the inability to control future experiences. They are then taken, either by way of enjoyment or of discontent and revolt, just as they come. Under such circumstances, it is idle to talk of self-control."[28]

In Dewey's view, "It may be a loss rather than a gain to escape from the control of another person only to find one's conduct dictated by immediate whim and caprice, that is, at the mercy of impulses into whose formation intelligent judgment has not entered. A person whose conduct is controlled in this way has at most only the illusion of freedom. Actually he is directed by forces over which he has no command."[29]

Thus, he held that an "overemphasis upon activity as an end, instead of upon intelligent activity, leads to identification of freedom with immediate execution of impulses and desires."[30]

TURNING DEWEY INSIDE OUT

Modern mass advertising is designed to equate freedom with the execution of impulses and desires. It turns Dewey's philosophy inside out. In the name of freedom and individuality, advertising encourages individuals to give in to their impulses. The result is that they are thus controlled more easily by others. The last thing in the world that advertisers want is for a target audience to have self-control. For Dewey, in contrast, freedom is expressed through the control of impulse in the service of intelligent purposes. To his mind, "The only freedom that is of enduring importance is freedom of intelligence, that is to say freedom of observation and of judgment exercised in behalf of purposes that are intrinsically worthwhile."[31]

In *Experience and Education,* Dewey described an educative experience as being part of a continuity of experiences that promote individual and community growth. Continuity of experience is, as he saw it, necessary both to provide context and meaning to immediate experiences and to shape subsequent experiences in the service of individual purposes. In his words, "when and *only* when development in a particular line conduces to continuing growth does it answer to the criterion of education as growing."[32] To Dewey, "Every experience is a moving force. Its value can be judged only on the ground of what it moves toward and into."[33] Furthermore, he explained, "No experience is educative that does not tend both to knowledge of more facts and entertaining of more ideas and to a better, a more orderly, arrangement of them."[34]

Dewey's educational philosophy rests on the belief that individuals are active members of real communities, which shape—and, in turn, are shaped by—them. In his words, "Every genuine experience has an active side which changes in some degree the objective experiences under which experiences are had."[35] In contrast, advertising deploys a variety of nonrational appeals and attempts to create pseudo communities based on consumption or the uncritical acceptance of a particular policy or point of view.

Educative experiences are the result of the interaction of the internal (or personal) and the external (or objective) in what Dewey termed a "situation." It is within the "situation" that the continuity of experience is made manifest, the individual and community changed, and the avenues of future growth created. Through this process, the individual advances in knowledge, self-control, and freedom, and the democratic community is progressively improved. Dewey explained that what is

learned in the way of knowledge and skill in one situation becomes an instrument of understanding and dealing effectively with the situations that follow. The process goes on as long as

> life and learning continue. . . . A fully integrated personality . . .
> exists only when successive experiences are integrated with one
> another. It can be built up only as a world of related objects is
> constructed. Continuity and interaction in their active union with
> each other provide the measure of the educative significance and
> value of an experience.[36]

Where Dewey seeks the integrative experiences in the service
of the individual and the community, advertising seeks to destroy
continuity and fragment experience, and encourages us to give
into our irrational impulses for the purpose of manipulating our
behavior.

The scope of modern advertising is almost impossible to
quantify. It might well be easier to identify those areas where
advertising is not present (there won't be many) than to document the volume of advertising unleashed on the American
public. In 1994, Leslie Savan estimated that television-watching
Americans see about 100 commercials a day. Add other commercial venues such as billboards, shopping carts, clothing
labels, and city buses, and the number of ads that clamor for
attention from each American reaches 16,000 a day.[37] One need
only consider the explosive growth of Web-based marketing over
the past decade to realize that, by now, the number is likely to
be much higher. There is little doubt that contemporary Americans live in an advertising-saturated environment and lead what
Savan termed "sponsored lives."

THE SPONSORED SCHOOLROOM

School is no different. Commercial activities now shape the structure of the school day, influence the content of the school
curriculum, and determine whether children have access to a
variety of technologies. Moreover, for a number of years marketers have been experimenting with bundling together advertising

and marketing programs in schools across a variety of media in an effort to gain a dominant position in the schoolhouse market. (Primedia, for example, owns Channel One and *Seventeen* magazine and has made various attempts at developing synergy in such relationships.) One of the most striking attempts at reaching into so many education-related industries, though, is Knowledge Universe, a complex investment organization founded by Michael Milken, the former "junk bond king" and convicted felon. With holdings in media, educational materials, schools, and training firms, "KU has a presence in virtually all aspects of play, education, and work," wrote Gerald Bracey in 2003.[38]

The impact of advertising on our personal lives and our communal relationships has been explored in a number of recent books such as *Stiffed: The Betrayal of the American Man*,[39] *Luxury Fever: Why Money Fails to Satisfy in an Era of Excess*,[40] *Deadly Persuasion: Why Women and Girls Must Fight the Addictive Power of Advertising*,[41] *Affluenza: The All-Consuming Epidemic*,[42] and *The Overspent American: Upscaling, Downshifting, and the New Consumer*.[43] Other recent books such as *Harvesting Minds: How TV Commercials Control Kids*,[44] *KinderCulture: The Corporate Construction of Childhood*,[45] and *Consuming Kids*[46] have addressed advertising's impact on children. The nature and impact of marketing in schools has been taken up, for example, in *Consuming Children: Education, Entertainment, Advertising*,[47] *Giving Kids the Business: The Commercialization of America's Schools*,[48] and *American Education and Corporations: The Free Market Goes to School*.[49]

COLONIZING OUR FUTURE

If the methods of modern mass marketing to adults threaten the happiness of individuals and undermine the well-being of our society, deploying them against children colonizes our future. No one can seriously suggest that children represent the rational consumer of market ideology; that is, children can in no sense be considered to have the same power, information, and freedom that adults are said to have to freely enter into contracts for goods and services in the idealized marketplace. Advertising to children is then a kind of immoral war on childhood, waged for the profit of adults who should be childhood's guardians. When advertising is conducted in schools, the immorality is compounded because the power of the state is twisted to the service of special interests, the ethical standing of educators is compromised, and the orientation of the school is shifted toward miseducative experiences.

When marketing firms find their way into the school—sponsoring programs, selling products, advertising their wares, or directly or indirectly contributing curriculum and other teaching materials—the ultimate outcome of their involvement is almost certain to be judged by the extent to which it meets the corporation's marketing objectives. This is especially clear in the case of sponsored curriculum materials: The firms that create such materials have to keep their corporate customers satisfied; their material is judged, first and foremost, by the extent to which it meets the objectives of their clients. The emphasis is not on providing the fullest and most accurate presentation of information to students, but on providing the spin that best suits corporate purposes. This fundamental difference between marketers and teachers distorts teaching as surely as a funhouse mirror distorts the image of anyone who looks into it. When teachers use propaganda developed by marketing firms instead of lessons taught to benefit students, the curriculum promotes the objectives of a third party whose interests may well conflict with those of the children, their families, and the country. Bernays might approve. Dewey would not.

If America's capacity to renew its democracy rests on an educated citizenry making well-informed public policy decisions, every American is poorly served when public schools turn their curricula into an educational flea market open to anyone who has the money to set up a table. Yet that is precisely what the relentless assault on funding for public education and repeated calls for "cooperation" with the business community are pushing schools to do.

In his book *Ghosts and the Curriculum*, Bill Doll suggests that the uneasy spirit of John Dewey "wanders the corridors of public education watching and waiting for his ideas to, at long last, be made flesh in the daily life of schools."[50] Doll dares to hope that the second millennium will belong to Dewey. All evidence, though, suggests that it is the spirits of Ivy Ledbetter Lee and Edward Bernays that are more likely to be happily at home in America's schools and classrooms this century than that of Dewey.

STRUGGLE, CORRUPTION, AND SILENCE

The current trend is not inevitable, as even marketers acknowledge. As early as September 1997, Matthew Klein in *Marketing Tools* warned advertisers that as far as school-based marketing programs go, "When a community feels a company has overstepped its bounds . . . no one is immune from the backlash." He went on to cite several examples: the backlash Campbell's experienced for sponsoring a phony science lesson designed to demonstrate that Campbell's Prego brand spaghetti sauce was thicker than its competitor's; the ban on sponsored textbook covers in a Staten Island school because of a father's outrage when his daughter came home with a temporary tattoo featuring a Calvin Klein logo; and the reexamination of all Seattle school district advertising as a result of efforts by the district administration to solicit paid advertising for its middle and high schools.[51]

Although the trend toward increased commercialism in the schools shows no signs of abating, concern about commercializing schools continues to grow. Editorial writers across the country have taken up the issue, among them CBS News radio commentator Dave Ross, who, responding to the rising trend of school bus advertising and other forms of commercialism, observed sarcastically: "I give you education's true purpose in two words: brand loyalty."[52]

Evidence of the potentially corrupting influence of commercial arrangements has repeatedly been reported. School officials, fearing the loss of funds from their corporate sponsors, resist efforts to cut back on corporate influence in education. In September 2004, the *Dallas Morning News* reported that a group funded by Coca-Cola—The Council for Corporate and School Partnerships—paid a $6,000 honorarium to the Dallas school district's then-superintendent, Mike Moses, during the same period in which Coke held an exclusive vending contract with the district.[53] In 2004, in New York City, Snapple won an exclusive contract to sell beverages in city buildings, including schools, in return for $40 million to the district for athletics and other activities, through what New York City Controller William Thompson called "a tainted process with a predetermined outcome that was not the best deal for the city of New York."[54] (Superintendent Joel Klein denied the accusation.[55]) The *New York Sun* related the account of an unidentified elementary school principal who refused to permit a Snapple vending machine in his school's lunchroom, despite pressure from a Snapple representative. A week after he turned away that representative, the principal was confronted with the delivery of two more machines, and with claims that there was a signed contract from the school principal—who had done no such thing. "This encounter was not unique," a union representative told the *Sun*. "Not all principals know that they can say no to Snapple," added Council of Supervisors and Administrators spokesman Richard Relkin. "And there are those who know that they can say no, but are too intimidated to do so." An anonymous principal told the newspaper that in a school such as his, where most children were on the free lunch program and already were provided with milk or juice, outside products posed several problems: pressure to spend money "that some of their parents can't really afford to give them," conflicts over money brought to school, and the likelihood of too much sugar even in purportedly healthful drinks.[56]

As a measure of how far short the professional education community is of John Dewey's ideals, it is telling that, despite the pervasiveness of schoolhouse commercialism, the education press has had very little to say about the issue.[57] At a time when commercialism in schools and classrooms is increasing dramatically, educators have been largely silent or, worse, cheerleaders for the trend. The failure of the education community to critically describe and attempt to understand and assess the impact of commercial activities on the character and quality of schools and their programs is not worthy of a profession that would lay claim to the legacy of John Dewey.

5

WHITTLE OR VIRTUALLY NOTHING: THE EMERGENCE OF EDISON SCHOOLS AND KNOWLEDGE UNIVERSE

A man named Christopher Whittle stands astride the path that leads from marketing *in* schools to the marketing *of* schools. In 1991, Whittle, a Nashville-based media entrepreneur, announced the creation of The Edison Project.[1] Whittle's Channel One television news service, launched in 1989, had quickly established itself in thousands of schoolrooms. Channel One piped ten minutes of televised news and two minutes of lucrative commercials into participating schools. It was the first major real-life test of a marketing model Whittle had conceived to link advertising with funding for public education. Whittle summarized that model in a 1988 address to the annual convention of the Eastern Tennessee Education Association: Schools represented a potential advertising medium worth perhaps $100 billion a year. If school officials would agree to accept "advertising sponsorship of teaching tools," Whittle said, "American teachers will soon have the best equipped, most modern classrooms in the world."[2] Channel One brought that vision to life: In return for participating schools' contractual guarantee of an audience of students, Channel One provided the free use of the television equipment necessary to beam the program into classrooms. And despite opposition in some communities, it initially grew quickly, reaching 12,000 schools by the mid-1990s, where it reached a plateau; by 2004, Channel One claimed to reach about 8 million students in 370,000 classrooms.[3]

EXIT CHANNEL ONE, ENTER THE EDISON PROJECT

Whittle's attempts to duplicate Channel One's success in venues other than schools failed. "Special Reports," carrying closed-circuit television commercials to patients in doctor's waiting rooms, and "Medical News Network," a similar venture aimed at doctors themselves. By 1994, Whittle Communications was hemorrhaging money and Whittle had been forced out of his job as chief executive officer by corporate partner Phillips Electronics, which then sold Channel One, the company's principal asset, to K-III Communications, later renamed Primedia Corp.[4]

Even as he was sinking money into "Special Reports" and "Medical News Network," Whittle set his sights on what he believed was a promising new venture: for-profit education. In 1991, Whittle had announced plans to launch a chain of for-profit private schools. The expanse of his ambition was reflected in the name he chose: The Edison Project. Just as lightbulb inventor Thomas Edison did not, according to Whittle, merely create a "better candle," so too the Edison Project schools would qualitatively transform schooling, the enthusiastic entrepreneur declared. Whittle set an equally ambitious goal: by 2000, he told interviewers, the Edison Project would operate a thousand private schools across the nation.[5] Private enterprise, he asserted, could wring huge efficiencies from the educational system and do a better job than public schools, teaching children with no additional money.[6]

Whittle's proposal coincided with a strong push for private school vouchers by Republican politicians and policy makers. Voucher programs would enable parents to use tax dollars to send their children to private schools. Originally proposed by Milton Friedman in the mid-1950s, vouchers were backed by a range of advocates, from free-market libertarians who contended that government should not be in the business of schooling children, to less radical advocates of "competition" as a tool to prod public schools to improve. A 1990 Wisconsin law creating a voucher program in Milwaukee limited to low-income families gave voucher advocates their first foot in the door. In Washington, meanwhile, the administration of President George H. W. Bush, although it failed to win passage of legislation, staked out a pro-voucher position.

Whittle denied that Edison's business plan depended on vouchers to succeed. Yet he seemed to have an inside track with voucher advocates such as Lamar Alexander, the elder Bush Administration's secretary of education. During his tenure as governor of Tennessee, Alexander had been a paid consultant to Whittle on education issues. Later, as president of the University of Tennessee, Alexander had transferred $10,000 in Whittle stock he owned to his wife, stock Whittle bought back for $330,000 a year later.[7]

EMBRACING THE MARKET

Whittle's knack for capturing the public eye helped set the Edison Project apart from other for-profit education ventures such as Education Alternatives, Inc. (EAI), launched in 1986. In 1992, Whittle announced the formation of a highly visible Edison Project "design team" that included, among others, free-market economist John Chubb and pro-voucher education ideologue Chester Finn. In May of that year he recruited Yale University President Benno Schmidt to run Edison as its CEO, which was news covered on the front page of the *New York Times*.[8] In the months that followed, generally enthusiastic stories on Whittle and his plans appeared in the *Chicago Tribune, Vanity Fair,* and *USA Weekend,* among others.[9]

Analysts who closely examined Edison's business premises were less enthusiastic. Denis P. Doyle, of the conservative Hudson Institute, declared of the prospect that Edison would turn a profit: "The likelihood of [that] is about zero."[10] Then came the 1992 elections. Democrat Bill Clinton defeated the first President Bush, and the possibility of federal support for vouchers evaporated.

The company's record over the next decade suggests that, notwithstanding Whittle's denials, Edison's original business plan *had* in fact relied on vouchers. In the aftermath of Clinton's victory and over the course of the next several years, Whittle refocused Edison's mission. Instead of attempting to create a network of private schools, which might have been eligible for publicly funded vouchers had the first Bush administration's goals been realized, Edison instead reconstituted itself as a manager of public schools and of public charter schools. Whittle's decision was made easier, no doubt, by Edison's precarious financial situation.

Charter schools, popularized by American Federation of Teachers President Al Shanker, were conceived as independent public schools, established by a body such as a group of teachers or parents or perhaps an academic institution, and operating under a "charter" granted by an agency such as a state, a city, or a school district. Central to the conception of charter schools was that they would be freed—in a way conventional public schools ostensibly were not—from purportedly onerous regulations. Joe Nathan, a University of Minnesota charter advocate, argued in 1996:

> The charter school idea is about the creation of more accountable public schools, and the removal of the "exclusive franchise" that local school boards presently have. Charter schools are public, nonsectarian schools that do not have admissions tests, but that operate under a written contract, or charter from a school board or some other organization, such as a state school board. These contracts specify how the school will be accountable for improved student achievement, in exchange for a waiver of most rules and regulations governing how they operate. Charter schools that improve achievement have their contracts renewed. Charter schools that do not improve student achievement over the contract's period are closed . . .
>
> The charter idea is not just about the creation of new, more accountable public schools or the conversion of existing public schools. The charter idea also introduces fair, thoughtful competition into public education.[11]

VOUCHERS FALL, CHARTERS RISE

With no support from the federal government during the 1990s, private school vouchers failed to win wide acceptance. Lengthy litigation over the legitimacy of the two existing experimental programs was one reason. Milwaukee's voucher program originally was limited to nonsectarian schools, but expanded to included religious schools in the mid-1990s. The Wisconsin Supreme Court in 1998 upheld the Milwaukee program's inclusion of religious schools on state constitutional grounds. The state's high court reasoned that, because voucher money was awarded to families rather than directly to schools, the law "will not have the primary effect of advancing religion."[12] In 1995, meanwhile, Ohio passed legislation appropriating state funds for the Cleveland Scholarship Program, which gave low-income Cleveland parents vouchers to attend private secular and religious schools. Providing tax dollars to religious schools through the program became the most publicized point of contention. Critics argued that permitting the use of publicly funded vouchers to attend religious schools violated the First Amendment separation of Church and State. In 2002, the U.S. Supreme Court upheld Cleveland's plan, ruling that the range of secular and religious schools available for parents to choose from meant that the plan did not violate the First Amendment prohibition against the establishment of religion.[13]

The U.S. Supreme Court ruling in the Ohio case has not as yet spurred significant growth in voucher programs. Voucher advocates suffered repeated defeats on ballot initiatives for more than 20 years, including lopsided negative votes in California and Michigan in 2000.[14] In state legislatures, meanwhile, voucher proposals have also fared poorly; in 2004 alone, voucher bills were defeated in 26 states, according to a lobbying group opposed to vouchers.[15] As a result, the number of new voucher programs has grown only slightly. In 1999, Florida established a program that makes students eligible for vouchers if they attend a school labeled "failing" by the state; it remains in effect amid a pending court challenge.[16] A second Florida program offers vouchers to disabled students.[17] Colorado passed a voucher law in 2003, only to see it struck down by the state Supreme Court in 2004.[18] In 2004, Congress established a voucher program for District of Columbia public school students.[19]

In contrast to the fierce resistance facing voucher schemes, charter schools have been largely embraced. With the encouragement and promotion of both President Bill Clinton and President George W. Bush, as of early 2004, 40 states and the District of Columbia had charter school laws on the books, and nearly 3,000 charter schools were in operation.[20] Indeed, it is charter schools in various forms, and not voucher schemes, that have become the primary vehicle by which for-profit education firms are attempting to create a private market in public education. The trajectory of Edison Schools illustrates the development.

EDISON CHANGES COURSE

Initially conceived as a company to run private schools, Edison shifted in the early 1990s toward managing public schools. As the decade progressed, Edison turned increasingly toward running charter schools. In 1999, Edison, originally founded as a privately held corporation, went public, opening on the New York Stock Exchange at $18 a share, then dropping to about $12 over the next few months. Enthusiasm from analysts who believed in the potential of an emerging "education industry," combined with Whittle's aggressive promotional publicity, helped push the company's value to nearly $38 a share in 2001, giving Edison executives enormous paper wealth.[21] At the same time, however, the public trading of its stock opened Edison's finances to public scrutiny. What investors and anyone else interested in the company's Security and Exchange Commission filings found was that Edison never turned a profit, and had little prospect of doing so. The company's share values fluctuated widely, often based on news reports of potential new contracts. By late 2002, Edison values had plummeted to as low as 14 cents a share. In 2003, Whittle took the company private, paying shareholders $1.76 a share.

From the time it signed a contract to manage its first school—the Renaissance Charter School in Boston in 1995—Edison grew steadily. Yet it was dogged by controversy over its treatment of special education students,[22] its academic performance,[23] its business practices,[24] and outright opposition from communities as far apart as San Francisco, New York, and Sherman, Texas.[25] In 2002, it won its largest-ever contract to manage twenty Philadelphia public schools, enrolling 13,000 students—a venture that illustrates the kind of notoriety and allegations of influence peddling Edison often generated.

EDISON'S PHILADELPHIA STORY

From the beginning, the circumstances under which the Philadelphia contract was awarded were contentious. In 2001, the Pennsylvania Department of Education, headed by Charles Zogby, awarded Edison a $2.7 million contract to analyze the needs of the Philadelphia district. There was widespread public suspicion that Edison's contract was a result of influence peddling. A subsequent audit by Pennsylvania Auditor General Robert P. Casey, Jr., concluded in August 2002 that the contract ignored state procurement laws.[26] In a follow-up report, Casey called the consulting agreement a "$2.7 million sweetheart deal" and asserted that no one had demonstrated why Edison was the most qualified firm to conduct the study.[27] That was only the beginning, however. In the political battle that ensued, Zogby resigned as Pennsylvania education secretary. (He went on to become a senior vice president at K12 Inc., a Virginia virtual charter school company chaired by William Bennett.)[28] Before resigning, Zogby used his authority to seek in court the removal of a three-member school board in Chester, Pennsylvania, in order to remove opposition to a state takeover of the Chester-Upland District and squelch criticism of Edison's performance running nine of the district's 10 schools.[29]

In sum, Pennsylvania's then-Governor Tom Ridge hired Edison, without competitive bidding, to evaluate Philadelphia schools.[30] Ridge's successor, Mark Schweiker, pushed through legislation dismantling Philadelphia's school board and creating an unelected governing board for the school district, and that body then awarded Edison a contract to run 20 of the district's schools.[31]

That contract, however, represented a disappointment to Edison. The firm had been expecting a larger share of the Philadelphia project, and, as a consequence, its stock had risen in the period of time preceding the contract.[32]

Edison's original premise held that the company could profit by offering better results than existing public schools with no additional resources. It was a premise always questioned by skeptics of for-profit education, and the company's Philadelphia experience flatly refuted the company's own claims. Edison repeatedly demanded more money and imposed cutbacks in resources.

UPPING THE ANTE

The ink was barely dry on the Philadelphia agreement when Edison sought $1,500 per pupil more than what the Philadelphia School District had provided; the company ultimately settled for half that amount to pay for teacher recruitment and professional development.[33] Almost immediately thereafter, Edison laid off 211 employees[34] and refused to take delivery on textbooks and supplies it had ordered, pleading poverty, despite an $11.8 million contract.[35]

And just how did Edison did save money? One way was to close school libraries, replacing them with a computerized test-taking drill system devised by Edison called Benchmarks. In 18 of Edison's 20 Philadelphia schools, the company established a lab where students in grades two through eight visited monthly to take the Benchmarks tests, answering questions on IBM computers designed to train them on Pennsylvania's statewide standardized tests.[36] An Edison official defended the switch away from libraries, saying test results could be used to give teachers "instant feedback" on what students were and were not learning so they could tailor instruction accordingly.[37]

Such language is central to the Edison image as a creative, rigorous, and innovative enterprise that would lift student achievement where conventional public schools have failed. For years, Edison has regularly produced accounts of its performance that claim improvement in the performance of schools it ran. Typical was the firm's 2003 annual report on the performance of its New Covenant Charter School in Albany, New York. There, Edison said, students increased their pass rate on the fourth grade tests by 6 percent in language and 29 percent in math.[38] Reporting on the performance of most of its schools in the nation, the company asserted in March 2003 that 84 percent of its schools had seen test scores improve "since they opened."[39] The announcement was just one of numerous press releases the company distributed at regular intervals over the years touting improved test scores. Another, in 2002, claimed "strong achievement gains" at schools targeted as in need of improvement by the federal No Child Left Behind Act.[40]

OUTSIDERS CRITIQUE EDISON

Outside observers, however, have generally found reason for far greater skepticism. The American Federation of Teachers called Edison's December 2002 data "misleading" and released its own report saying that, despite improvements, Edison schools' students consistently underperformed their counterparts at similar public schools.[41] Individual communities also took exception to Edison's claims. In the Chester Upland district in Pennsylvania, where a state takeover of the district put Edison in charge of nine schools, test scores fell in all nine by the fall of 2002.[42] Edison dismissed the results as "baseline scores ... that reflect the historically low performance of the district."[43] Yet Chester Upland was far from alone.

A year after Edison touted improved performance at Albany's New Covenant Charter School, comparisons between that school's 2004 test scores and those of nearby Arbor Hill Elementary School favored Arbor Hill. That was despite the fact that Arbor Hill's poverty rate, an indicator consistently associated with lower test scores, was higher than New Covenant's.[44] An examination of Edison in 2002 by the General Accounting Office (GAO; now called the Government Accountability Office) shed little light on the matter, concluding that, notwithstanding earlier critical studies of Edison schools' performance, there simply was not enough information to show whether for-profit education companies were effective.[45]

Edison has repeatedly been found to make questionable, indeed at times misleading, claims about its test scores. In its May 18, 2004, press release, Edison asserted that test score gains at its Michigan schools were "six times greater" than average annual local and state gains, but did not offer direct comparisons between comparable schools.[46]

Not surprisingly, the company's costs and its disappointing performance produced widespread dissatisfaction. Some schools and districts cancelled contracts. In 2002 alone, at least six of Edison's contracts were cancelled because of high costs, failure to raise test scores, or both.[47] Among the most dramatic was in Dallas, Texas, where the school district cancelled the company's contract to run seven schools after just two years, noting that the company's schools performed no better than other comparable schools and cost 10 percent more to run.[48] Similar complaints have surfaced across the country, and repeatedly have called into question Edison's record for improving student achievement. In Clark County, Nevada, Edison took over management of seven schools early in the decade when two were on the state's list of "inadequate" schools (as measured by test scores). By 2003, the Nevada Assembly's education committee chairman, Wendell Williams, noted that in the wake of Edison's management, six of the seven schools had wound up on the list.[49] After the Wichita, Kansas, school district took back two schools that had been run by Edison, the schools' academic performance improved markedly.[50]

DISAPPOINTING PERFORMANCE

Such problems aren't unique to Edison-run schools. Since the for-profit industry now seems to be driving the growth of charter schools, the performance of charter schools provides another rough gauge of the industry's ability to improve educational achievement. Across the country, the studies and evaluations available find that charter schools sometimes perform about as well as traditional public schools, occasionally better, but more often worse. One such examination was conducted by the American Federation of Teachers (AFT), which reviewed data from the National Assessment of Educational Progress (NAEP) and concluded in August 2004 that charter school students were performing less well than their traditional public school counterparts, which caused an explosion of outrage among charter supporters.[51] Nevertheless, a U.S. Department of Education comparison of charter school and conventional public school performance in five states, released in November 2004, largely confirmed the AFT findings. The Department of Education found that charters fell short of their counterparts in meeting state performance standards.[52] In Texas, for example, fully 98 percent met such requirements in 2002, compared with 66 percent of charters. Similar trends were found in Colorado, Illinois, Massachusetts, and North Carolina.[53] The study, it should be noted, was commissioned in 1998 by the Clinton administration; after its completion under the Bush administration, it was not made public until the *New York Times* filed a Freedom of Information Act request to compel its release.

Pro-charter and pro-voucher advocates have greeted such studies defensively. Eight days after the *New York Times* ran a story about the August AFT report on the front page, a group of social scientists and charter supporters organized by the pro-charter Center for Education Reform signed a full page ad in the *Times* criticizing it—a rapid, and expensive, response. Reacting to the study released in November 2004, one charter and voucher advocate, Harvard University's Paul Peterson, defended charter schools' poorer performance by taking note that many charter schools enrolled high proportions of poor minority students: "When you have targeted a needy population, you will have more difficulty reaching state standards."[54] Such a defense, however, contrasts starkly with the criticisms levied at public schools. Among the privatization activists, no such allowance is made for supposedly "failing" inner-city schools where 100 percent of students are from families living at or below the poverty level. Indeed, an August 2004 report by Jay Greene and Greg Forster, of the pro-voucher Manhattan Institute, sought to dismiss the evidence of the impact of poverty on student achievement.[55]

WHO'S IN CHARGE HERE?

It's a common argument in favor of charter schools to portray them as mechanisms for giving greater control to teachers, parents, and community members. As the for-profit industry in general, and large, for-profit firms such as Edison, White Hat Management, and others in particular, control an ever-larger portion of the charter school sector, this argument is becoming more rhetorical flourish than practical reality. Indeed, Edison's practices, for example, may be driving many teachers away. In Springfield, Illinois, the company abandoned what had been one of its principal selling points when it won the contract to manage the Feitshans-Edison school: longer school days and longer school years. In 2003, the district allowed Edison to shorten its school year to 190 days from 200 and its school day to 7 hours and 15 minutes from 8 hours, after the company complained of declining attendance in the summertime and attrition of teachers seeking jobs in districts with shorter hours and calendars.[56]

To be sure, the issues of charter school performance and Edison's performance are not the same thing. Edison's spotty performance and its history of inflating and mischaracterizing its results are not by themselves a basis for passing judgment on charter schools. Indeed, the company's academic performance problems can be found across the board—not only in its charter schools, but in the conventional schools it manages. Separately, but at the same time, broader examinations of charter schools have failed to find that they improve achievement overall, notwithstanding successes at some individual charters. Therefore, the lackluster performance of charter schools in raising achievement, and the problems that for-profit school management companies like Edison have experienced, together call into question the wisdom of shutting down "failing" traditional public schools and offering students charter schools, because the charter schools may very well be worse—especially if they are managed by for-profit firms.

EDISON UNDER FIRE

Questions about Edison's academic performance questions led inevitably to questions about its long-term financial prospects. In 2002, as Edison's share prices collapsed, state education officials and individual schools in Michigan;[57] Albany, New York;[58] and Maryland[59] demanded that the company prepare contingency plans for the operation of its schools in the event of a corporate failure. The Philadelphia School District filed legal papers to protect property in the 20 schools Edison was running from being claimed by creditors in the event of bankruptcy.[60] In May 2002, the Securities and Exchange Commission issued an order criticizing the company for overstating revenues (by claiming as revenue teacher salaries school districts paid to teachers in the company's schools).[61] Shareholders reacted by suing both Edison and its accounting firm, Pricewaterhouse-Coopers.[62]

In the meantime, the company also came under fire from unions. The Service Employees International Union, which represents janitors in many public schools, circulated a memo urging pension funds not to invest with Leeds, Weld and Co., an investment group that included former Massachusetts Governor William Weld, a school privatization advocate.[63] The union complained about what it said was the harm Edison did to public schools and their employees. (Leeds, Weld later pulled out of Edison investments, saying "it no longer believes that companies managing schools for profit can make enough money to justify the political risk of investing in them."[64])

Reflecting the growing skepticism about Edison's prospects, *Fortune* magazine in December 2002 asserted that "Edison doesn't work." Central to the magazine's assessment was a conclusion familiar to long-time Edison critics. While Edison had initially targeted middle-class students, the company's real customers were inner-city schools serving the disadvantaged—students whom it cost far more to teach.[65] Because profit margins were low and economies of scale that the Edison "visionaries" had imagined proved to be largely illusory, *Fortune* argued, "for-profit education just isn't a very good business."[66] The magazine concluded, "For-profit schools have to be orders of magnitude better than their public school rivals in order to overcome the political opposition that confronts them. And so far that hasn't happened."[67]

EDISON GOES PRIVATE

Amid continued turmoil, Edison in 2002 shifted away from its fast-growth business strategy. The company also gave up on what had been its core selling point—the claim that it could outdo public school administrators without more money. The story of the Chester Upland District in Pennsylvania offers a snapshot. As noted earlier, Chester Upland was forced to contract with Edison to run nine schools after a state takeover of the district in 2001.[68] Under Edison, scores fell in 2002,[69] yet Edison threatened to withdraw and nearly doubled its fee to $4.4 million a year, telling officials "that if they want better schools, they must pay for them."[70] (That same year the company dropped 14 contracts worth $37 million in yearly revenues on which it had lost $765,000.[71]) The Chester Upland District agreed to renew Edison's contract,[72] then saw the district's budget deficit soar to $13 million in less than two years, in part because of the costs Edison imposed.[73] By early 2005, sentiment had shifted against Edison among school leaders, with a majority of the school board urging the cancellation of the company's contract, and the interim superintendent calling for the contract not to be renewed in 2006.[74]

During Edison's four years as public company from 1999 to 2003, its financial woes persisted. By the end of 2002 the company was predicting it would be profitable for the first time in the upcoming fourth quarter.[75] Yet the day after Edison reported in May 2003 that it had accomplished "a dramatic financial turnaround," the company quietly revealed in an SEC filing that it was in default on loans totaling $59.5 million.[76] By mid-2003, Whittle and other senior managers at Edison had little choice but to take the company private.[77] In July, Whittle announced that he would buy out the firm at $1.76 a share with Liberty Partners, a private equity firm, financing the transaction.[78]

This arrangement also generated controversy. Liberty Partners is a New York City investment firm that managed the $1.8 billion (assets) Florida Retirement System. The transaction, valued at $174 million with the assumption of debt included, gave Liberty 96.3 percent of Edison—and it used Florida's retirement funds as its sole source of cash for the project. The deal drew immediate fire from teacher representatives and others in Florida. They argued that Edison's track record financially (losses of $354 million over 12 years) made it an unsound investment for state retirement funds, and that the company itself threatened the jobs of public employees.[79] Meanwhile, lawyers representing shareholders filed a total of seven lawsuits, alleging that the price was inadequate.[80] A class-action settlement was reached in June 2004, awarding the plaintiffs $5.4 million.[81]

EDISON DIVERSIFIES

Even as Edison went private, the company continued to change its strategy away from large-scale school management projects, as in Philadelphia, to managing public schools in medium-sized markets. In larger cities, Whittle said, Edison would focus on charter schools rather than on management contracts for conventional public schools.[82] And Edison continues to make other changes in its business plan, diversifying into an array of ancillary businesses. On its Web site, the company now lists a broad array of services that make up its education business. In addition to its core business of managing public and public charter schools, Edison's activities include providing private tutoring; operating summer schools; providing test preparation services and programs; selling curriculum materials; offering in-service training for teachers; and Edison Alliance, which the firm describes as "a customized service that is dedicated to helping schools and districts improve achievement and meet AYP targets"—that is, targets for Annual Yearly Progress under the federal No Child Left Behind Act.[83]

In early 2003, the company announced plans to market Benchmark Assessments as part of a new Achievement Management Solutions product line targeting schools seeking to raise their test scores in compliance with the law.[84]

Edison may see summer schooling as another ripe target. In November 2002, the company said it would rapidly expand summer school and after-school divisions.[85] Such an expansion would, no doubt, be to some degree in response to the No Child Left Behind Act and its requirement for annual testing of all students. In another sign that Edison is maneuvering into summer schooling, Edison officials in 2003 joined school superintendents and the Missouri School Boards' Association in campaigning against a legislative proposal in Missouri to abolish a financial bonus for summer school students that boosted state aid to local school districts. By allowing districts to count summer school students twice when reporting attendance figures on which state aid is based, the bonus gives school districts a financial incentive that has driven up summer school enrollment. High enrollment, in turn, led some districts to hire Edison to run summer schools, and to promote attendance, Edison has used incentives such as bicycles, video games, stereos, and gift certificates.[86]

THE FLAW IN FOR-PROFIT MANAGEMENT

It is clear that for-profit management companies are a driving factor in charter school growth, and that large firms in the industry are driving the growth of for-profit school management. Both trends are certain to magnify the fundamental problem with for-profit management of charter schools, or indeed of any public school: namely, the underlying assumption that schools can be adequately operated with existing resources, with money left over for investors. Its advocates insist that for-profit management will not sacrifice school quality in pursuit of higher returns. Edison's own actions—demanding higher payments and dropping contracts of schools it cannot "afford" to operate—suggest otherwise. At the same time, however, Edison in 2004 undertook an advertising campaign, primarily in *Education Week*.[87] The very existence of this campaign underscores that for-profit companies operating schools can be expected to do what most for-profit companies do: spend money on sales and marketing, money that otherwise could be used to direct additional resources to the very schools Edison has complained it cannot afford to run at the rates to which it originally agreed.

While Edison has become the most widely discussed example of school privatization, it is by no means the only firm in the market. In less than a decade, the number of for-profit, so-called education management companies profiled annually by the Education Policy Studies Laboratory at Arizona State University has grown more than fourfold, from 13 in 1998–1999 to 59 in 2004–2005.

A number of firms, employing business models very different from Edison's, have generally sought and received much less attention. Some, such as National Heritage Academies and White Hat Management, have managed to grow steadily.[88] National Heritage, based in Grand Rapids, Michigan, has grown from 14 schools in its home state in 1998 to 31 schools enrolling 20,000 students in five states in 2003. White Hat, based in Akron, Ohio, has grown from 12 Ohio schools in 1999 to 30 schools enrolling more than 6,000 students in Ohio and Arizona in 2003.

FOR-PROFIT SCHOOLING RESHAPES ITSELF

As with any maturing industry, the education management industry has seen failure and consolidation. Education Alternatives, Inc., which preceded Edison, underwent a remarkably similar trajectory early on. Originally founded as a network of private schools, EAI converted to a manager of public and public charter schools. It later renamed itself TesseracT Schools, and ultimately went out of business in 2000. Mosaica acquired Advantage Schools in 2001, and Chancellor Academies and Beacon

Education Management combined to form Chancellor Beacon Academies in early 2002, later renaming itself Imagine Schools.

For the majority of these companies, however, charter school legislation has been the principal framework under which they operate.[89] Almost all of these companies are privately held, and thus it is impossible to know whether the business of running schools is profitable for them, except by their own self-report or by the grossest measure of success or failure: whether they continue to operate or not.

THE RISE OF VIRTUAL SCHOOLS

The latest development among for-profit and charter schools is the creation of "virtual" charter schools. Such schools typically use the Web to link home-based students with education programs, and in turn collect state funds ordinarily directed to public schools. *Profiles of For-Profit Education Management Companies 2003–2004* identified at least four profit-seeking companies operating 17 such virtual schools enrolling at least 10,530 students in 11 states.[90] Other sources have indicated higher estimates. For instance, a *Los Angeles Times* article in January 2003 counted six virtual-charter providers (both for-profit and nonprofit) in California,[91] and a *Chicago Tribune* article in 2002 calculated that 16,000 students were enrolled in charter schools in 12 states "with some element of online study."[92]

To open the door to the operation of virtual schools, state legislatures have generally had to enact enabling legislation. A series of searches on the news database Nexis, conducted in mid-2004 and going back to 2000, found a total of seventy pieces of legislation that were in some way connected with enabling or establishing online public school options.

Online education has been called "the next wave in technology-based K–12 education."[93] Journalists such as *U.S. News and World Report* writer Mary Lord have praised the trend, suggesting it as a solution for students victimized by bullies among other problems, while noting that learning alone online "demands the self-discipline to work independently, a trait many children may lack."[94]

Although such schools require no new buildings or other infrastructure beyond online software, charter arrangements generally have allowed them to collect the same amount of state money per pupil support as so-called bricks-and-mortar schools. In Ohio, for example 10 online charter schools accounted in 2003 for about 20 percent of the state's charter school students, with for-profit companies White Hat Management Co., Altair Learning, and K12 Inc. operating three of them.[95] In Appleton, Wisconsin, Sylvan Learning Systems and the Appleton Area School District started up the similarly structured Wisconsin Connections Academy in the 2002–2003 school year.[96] (In July 2003, Educate Inc. took ownership of Sylvan Learning Systems' K–12 business in a $282 million management-led buyout and formed Connections Academy Inc. as a division.[97])

In Arizona, Chancellor Beacon Academy formed a partnership with Connections Academy to operate Chancellor Arizona Connections Academy (CA2), one of five so-called schools without walls. CA2 was touted as using certified teachers, "community experiences," and technology to teach children needing "an individualized approach to education."[98] Students enrolled would study at home and "attend" classes via a home computer.[99]

WILLIAM BENNETT AND K12 INC.

The company with the highest profile in this field, however, is K12 Inc., founded and led by former Reagan Administration U.S. Education Secretary William Bennett. In 2003, with contracts already in eight states, Bennett's firm bucked a trend of declining investment in for-profit education, obtaining $20 million in financing in April 2003.[100] K12 Inc. works on two separate marketing tracks. On the one hand, it provides proprietary, Web-based curriculum materials marketed for homeschoolers, having enrolled about 2,000 in the first few years of its operation. Separately, however, it has aggressively pursued, and benefited from, passage of virtual school legislation. Its core business strategy entails forming partnerships with public schools and then being paid with state funds under charter or online education laws.[101] Its two markets—homeschooled children and public school children—overlap when homeschooled children are "enrolled" in virtual schools; this makes the curriculum free to them and assigns the cost of homeschooling to the state, thus increasing educational costs.

Press releases from K12 outline its marketing tactic: hosting free, daylong "Expos" with speakers, including Bennett, discussing the company's approach.[102] Such Expos around the country have helped pave the way for the company's expansion. In a typical arrangement, the company formed a partnership with the Northern Ozaukee School District in Wisconsin to start the Wisconsin Virtual Academy in the 2003–2004 school year.[103]

CRITICISM OF VIRTUAL SCHOOLING

Virtual charter schools have not been universally welcomed, however. Some homeschooling advocates, for example, are highly critical of K12, fearing the company's charter arrangements will put homeschoolers under state control.[104] Attempts to start two virtual charter schools in central New York failed in 2002 and 2003.[105] Rejecting one such attempt, which would have been managed by K12 Inc., the State University of New York in 2002 contended that a school without a physical site did not meet state legal requirements for charter schools.[106] That plan failed for two reasons: School districts balked at the $7,800-per-pupil cost, skeptical because there was no infrastructure other than the provision of free computers and printers to enrollees. "It looks like an absolute windfall for the charter-school operator," a county school official told the newspaper *Newsday* in early 2003.[107] Moreover, homeschooling parents didn't support it. Objections included a requirement that enrollees in the virtual charter eventually take the New York State Regents' exams, and the fear that taking public money would subject this group of homeschoolers to government regulation.[108] Columbia University Education Professor Luis Huerta points out the problem for state policy makers: "Promoting the common good may be difficult, if not impossible, given the vague state legislation that has allowed the VCS [virtual charter schools] to operate in such an autonomous environment."[109]

THE MILKEN CONNECTION, AND OTHER MUSCLE

K12 Inc. is backed by a $20 million investment from a group led by Constellation Ventures and has backing as well from Knowledge Universe, an education investment operation run by former junk bond king and convicted felon Michael Milken.[110] Despite, or perhaps because of, its deep pockets and its aggressive growth, K12 Inc. has found itself under fire. Lawsuits in Minnesota and Wisconsin have challenged online schools in which K12 Inc. is a partner.[111] In a Minnesota lawsuit filed October 9, 2003, Education Minnesota, the state's largest teachers union, challenged the legality of state funding for an online school operated by the small, rural, Houston, Minnesota, school district using the K12 Inc. curriculum. Education Minnesota alleged in its lawsuit that the program failed to provide adequate supervision by state-certified teachers, in violation of Minnesota law.[112] Coplaintiffs included two Minneapolis-area school districts, who argued that state funding of Houston's program threatened their own online school plans.[113] A lawsuit filed January 7, 2004, by the Wisconsin Education Association Council similarly challenged the legality of the Wisconsin Virtual Academy, an online school run by K12 in partnership with the Northern Ozaukee (Wisconsin) School District.[114] That suit, which was pending in late 2004, challenged the district's enrollment of students from outside its boundaries in the program, and the use of nonlicensed instructors such as the students' parents. The union alleged that the academy would receive $5,500 for each of 420 students, or $2.3 million.[115]

Despite such challenges, K12 Inc. has shown considerable political muscle. In Idaho, when a Republican state senator, Gary Schroeder, launched an investigation into K12 Inc. and the Idaho Virtual Academy in mid-2004, he found himself under attack by a pro-K12 political action group, Idahoans for Tax Reform. Schroeder charged the group with conducting misleading and distorting "polls" of voters to suppress votes for him in an upcoming election. The state senator charged that K12 Inc. had bullied the legislature into paying out an additional $1.6 million for the virtual charter by threatening to close, and that the company's political allies had targeted him for defeat because of his role as chairman of the state Senate Education Committee.[116] Meanwhile, Idaho's State Board of Education came under fire for an agreement with K12 that kept its profit margins secret, despite its being paid with state tax dollars.[117]

HIGH-TECH IDEA, LOW-TECH RESULTS

Virtual charters have produced skepticism in some quarters. Trinity University's Education Department chairman, Paul Kelleher, said in a 2003 newspaper interview that the concept appears to heighten the risk that some children would get inadequate schooling.[118] The Texas Senate passed a bill that would have permitted taxpayer-funded virtual charter schools, but the state House of Representatives defeated similar legislation.[119] A report at CBS MarketWatch.com—while directed at consumers who may pay for online schooling themselves—offers reasons to be wary of taxpayer-funded virtual schooling. Andrea Coombes, the writer, advised readers that before committing to an online course, "Find out who will be teaching the class."[120] An educational telecommunications consultant told Coombes: "It's one thing to have a university like Stanford or Johns Hopkins, it's another thing to have a private for-profit company that may not have certified or qualified folks doing the material. Check out every angle first."[121] And one educator's analysis of K12's primary school curriculum left her singularly unimpressed with its emphasis on violent events and memorization, and its poor use of technology. Noting K12 founder Bennett's high profile as a contemporary American moralist, the analyst, Susan Ohanian, writes:

> Yet the K12 curriculum, relentless in its presentation of map skills, warriors, and the hierarchy of the Catholic Church, rarely provides a moral message about some of the appalling historical events it includes. . . . First graders get the Trojan War, with the objectives of the lesson being: Find Greece on the map of ancient Greece. Find Troy. Identify Priam as the King of Troy. Identify Odysseus as a Greek hero. That's it. Greek and Roman myths provide the "story" in "history": tales of incest, rape, and murder. No moral comment is provided, other than to remind children that this is fiction, not fact. Throughout the curriculum, history is stripped of moral import and objectified as discrete facts to be memorized.[122]

There is no evidence, Ohanian points out, that either the public schools serving as charter sponsors of K12's program, or the state education agencies under whose ultimate authority the company operates, have made any assessment of the quality of its curriculum.[123]

She is not alone in her criticism. Elliot Soloway of the University of Michigan criticized the company's use of worksheet-style computer lessons that rewarded right answers with sound effects and animated clips, and told *Education Week,* "In the twenty-first century, they're delivering a nineteenth-century curriculum."[124] A Wisconsin parent told the *New York Times,* "Young kids are being encouraged through technology to run a maze, ring a bell, and eat the cheese."[125]

To the extent that virtual charters benefit anyone, an advocate, Mary Lord, unwittingly put her finger on why they may simply help the rich get richer in educational terms—allowing those already likely to succeed in any educational setting to zoom ahead, while doing little or nothing to help the most at-risk disadvantaged students: "A supportive home environment and involved parents also are key."[126]

WASHINGTON: PRIVATIZATION'S FRIEND

As private corporations consolidate and expand their reach into the management of public and public charter schools, the federal government's response has been mixed. On the one hand, the U.S. Education Department has on some occasions cracked down, as in 2003, when a federal inspector general's audit of the Arizona Education Department concluded that the state agency improperly gave more than $1.1 million in federal money to charter schools run by for-profit companies, and recommended requiring the state to repay the funds. Tom Horne, the state superintendent objected to the audit's conclusions, contending that all charter schools were "public schools" by definition and therefore qualified for the funds. Horne said he would appeal the audit's findings.[127] (A review of the state and federal education departments' Web sites in late 2004 indicated no new developments in the dispute.)

Despite a restrictive federal stance toward for-profit education in the Arizona finding, however, the Bush administration has pushed education privatization while being widely criticized for underfunding No Child Left Behind (NCLB). On November 18, 2003, People for the American Way released the report

"Funding a Movement: U.S. Department of Education Pours Millions into Groups Advocating School Vouchers and Education Privatization." It cited a total of $77 million awarded over three years in the form of grants to organizations including K12 Inc., the pro-voucher Black Alliance for Educational Options, and the Center for Education Reform, among others.[128]

The step-by-step reach of for-profit corporations into the management of public schools and public charter schools has been enabled by and at the same time has helped feed an important shift in the public's perceptions. A generation ago, the notion of a for-profit company managing a public school almost certainly would have been dismissed as inherently unworkable and indeed undesirable. Public schools were public institutions, directed by duly elected representatives of the public.

Private entities have succeeded in framing the debate and their role as one of rescuing public schools, not harming them, and have managed to persuade many—in defiance of simple logic—that it would be possible to manage public schools in the public interest while doing so for the private profit of investors.

CHARTERS: PRIVATIZATION'S VEHICLE

To charter school proponents, the fact that charters exist is sometimes taken as evidence of their value, because they believe that charters create for students competition that pushes traditional public schools toward improvement. Advocates also point to increased parental choice as an unqualified good. Add to the list the promise of accountability for improving student achievement, and charters seem like a pretty good deal. As charter advocate Joe Nathan wrote in the mid-nineties, "If we can't improve student achievement, close down our schools." The list of charter school promises was attractive enough to the authors of the federal NCLB Act that they made charters a solution to the problem of chronically "failing" schools.

Thus, charter school legislation and the virtual school laws that followed have become, in large measure, the legal framework for the expansion of the for-profit education management industry. Operating for the most part outside of effective governmental oversight, large for-profit firms such as Edison Schools, White Hat Management, and Chancellor Beacon Academies now enroll the bulk of students attending for-profit charter schools. The more traditional public schools that are labeled "failing" under the terms of the No Child Left Behind Act, the more money these companies stand to make. Any potential threat to the NCLB charter school provision is, therefore, a threat to their bottom line.

This raises the possibility that at least some of the vocal support for charter schools may be more about dollars than student achievement. It is instructive that only a few months before the Center for Education Reform (CER) sponsored the *New York Times* ad that so loudly defended charter schools in the face of evidence to the contrary, CER's head, Jeanne Allen, signed on as the lobbyist for the newly formed for-profit education industry trade group, the National Council of Education Providers.[129] In her role as head of the Center for Education Reform, Allen has long argued for less regulation of charters. In assuming the role of the for-profit sector's paid lobbyist, she must be seen as serving the interests of her lobbying clients, and the Center for Education Reform's agenda must be questioned.

Allen's transformation is an apt metaphor for an entire industry. Education companies are selling themselves as reformers, but they are in fact lobbyists. While they purport to advocate reforms in the public interest, they in fact lobby for self-serving advantage. Increasingly, the concept of the charter school—once conceived as a community-based, voluntary institution driven primarily by parents and teachers—has become conflated in practice and in the public mind with for-profit companies. The emergence of virtual schools driven by companies such as K12 completes that arc. Thanks to the low-cost business model of a school that can deliver an inexpensive curriculum without maintaining the cost of a school building, virtual charters may in fact accomplish what their brick-and-mortar predecessors only dreamed of: being able to pocket significant profits from the public tax dollars they collect.

6

FUTURES TRADING: BUYING AND SELLING EDUCATION IN THE GLOBAL MARKETPLACE

Corporations have found in schools a uniquely powerful vehicle for advertising their products: one that delivers a captive audience of children. Moreover, they have conflated every aspect of school with their own interests in selling products, consumerist values, and corporation-friendly ideas. Even public education itself is now up for sale.

Corporations teach our children directly through self-serving curricula, and indirectly through everything from fund-raising schemes to in-school marketing and advertising campaigns. With notable exceptions, educators' reactions range from tacit acceptance to outright embrace of their actions. Virtually every corporate marketing program tied to the public school system is linked by a common thread: the schools' need for resources beyond those available through conventional funding mechanisms. This is true whether the corporate marketing activity in question involves direct fund-raising (through sales programs sponsored by schools or by parent–teacher groups), exclusive agreements in which soft drink bottlers pay premiums and bonuses to schools, or the sponsorship of specific school programs. It is also true in the case of activities such as sponsored curricula, which schools accept presumably because they perceive it to fill gaps in their existing teaching materials. It is true in the case of Channel One, the in-school television network, whose programming schools accept because they want access to the proffered "free" television equipment.

In much the same way, programs that directly privatize instruction and schooling have grown in large part because they are perceived to address a resource gap. Privately managed charter schools appeal to parents who see in them promoted features, such as small classes and purportedly innovative curriculum, without having to pay extra. Where they have been established, private school voucher programs are perceived to provide similar advantages to schoolchildren and their parents. Virtual charter schools add the lure of one-on-one individualized instruction.

Thus it is that selling *to* schools and selling *in* schools are only two forms taken by the market as it transforms public education. The third form—the selling *of* schools—privatization—transforms public education into a segmented collection of private products and services sold for the profit of investors.

Privatization of schools, in this respect, is similar to the leveraged buyout of companies in the private sector. In this instance, the school's resources (tax dollars) are used to acquire control of the school, which is then divided into profit centers that can be sold off (contracted out) or operated by the management firm, depending on which option is most profitable.

PUTTING SCHOOLS TO THE TEST:
NO CHILD LEFT BEHIND

It was a rare moment of bipartisan unity in 2002 when President George W. Bush invited Senator Ted Kennedy to an Ohio high school for the signing of the bill reauthorizing the Elementary and Secondary Education Act (ESEA) of 1965. A key promise from Bush's 2000 campaign for president, the reauthorization was given the name "No Child Left Behind"—or NCLB for short. The act contained an unprecedented provision: If schools fell short of federally mandated increases in achievement test scores, state education departments were given the authority to close schools, fire their staffs, hire new principals and teachers, or transform them into charter schools.

NCLB for the first time put in place a national requirement for schools to test students in grades three through eight and show certain test score results in return for federal aid. Every school must show "Adequate Yearly Progress" (AYP) in its test scores, and in addition to meeting the AYP threshold for the student body as a whole, schools must demonstrate it for individual categories of students: minority group members, special education students, and students for whom English is a second language. Initially, schools that fall short of the AYP standard may be subject to losing federal funds.

No Child Left Behind calls for *all* students in *all* schools to achieve a "proficient level" on state achievement tests within twelve years. The first tests given were in reading and math. Science tests will be added in 2006. In addition to state achievement tests, NCLB requires that all students participate every other year in the National Assessment for Education Progress, an exam designed to gauge the overall performance of American students in reading, science, math, and other subjects. Parents of children enrolled in schools that fail to meet NCLB's achievement requirements are given the right to enroll their children in schools with better test scores and in after-school remedial programs funded by tax dollars.

As originally proposed, NCLB would have enabled those parents to enroll their children in private schools with taxpayer funding. Strong congressional opposition to vouchers forced the removal of that provision. Nevertheless, the law establishes charter schools as a remedy for schools labeled failing and thus creates a legal mechanism for promoting privatization.

A SOLUTION WORSE THAN THE PROBLEM

The relentless testing and accountability regime applied to public schools is deeply problematic if the end result is creating more taxpayer-funded for-profit charter schools. To date, there is little in the performance of schools managed by for-profit firms that would justify offering them as a solution for the problem of "failing" schools.

Even as Education Management Organizations (EMOs) point to test scores as evidence of their success, critics find serious flaws in their data. In August 2002, the for-profit company Edison Schools released test scores for its San Francisco charter elementary school. The scores "inexplicably inflated scores in all 16 categories from 2 to 9 percentile points," reported Parents Advocating School Accountability, a group critical of the company, citing the company's own publicity statements and the scores as posted on the California Department of Education's Web site.[1] Earlier the same year, Edison publicity material quoted the RAND Corporation as reporting that 84 percent of its schools made "positive gains" in 2000–2001. RAND researchers, however, responded that they had not completed their evaluations of Edison and were not yet in a position to report any results.[2]

These incidents help illustrate how, over the past decade, for-profit education management companies have grown and attracted investment dollars and new contracts in part by exaggerating their performance.[3]

For-profit education management companies have also tended to grow because of their political connections. For instance, Advantage Schools' founder Steve Wilson helped write the Massachusetts charter school law when he was an aide to former Governor William Weld.[4] An Edison-run school in Milwaukee won support from the city's pro-voucher, pro-charter mayor for a $12.1 million tax-exempt bond issue, despite its troubled start.[5] White Hat Management in Ohio has benefited repeatedly from exceptions in the laws and policies governing that state's charter schools; the company's founder and CEO, David Brennan, contributed $1 million to Republican legislators and other office holders.[6]

The industry's history of scandals suggests that there is no real basis for regarding for-profit management as the "solution" to "failed" public schools. Despite the industry's checkered record, however, for-profit school management companies continue to benefit from their political connections and the prevailing ideology of privatization.

In addition to for-profit school management, No Child Left Behind, with its emphasis on testing, has created a niche market for test-coaching services. Private companies have also begun to market after-school and summer school tutoring programs eligible for federal payment under the act. Edison Schools is, for example, marketing a product line, Achievement Management Solutions, that targets schools seeking to raise school test scores.[7] As noted earlier, the company has expanded beyond its core school management business to offer private tutoring; operate summer schools; provide test preparation services and programs; sell curriculum materials; offer in-service training for teachers; and, through Edison Alliance, help schools and districts meet their NCLB AYP targets.[8]

A *Baltimore Sun* investigation of educational software offered by firms seeking to cash in on NCLB funding found that the companies promoted themselves

> ... by telling struggling schools across the country they can comply with its [NCLB's] tough standards by buying the companies' products. In pitches often sweetened with dinner cruises and other perks, software vendors make sweeping claims for computer programs and online networks that promise to assess students' weaknesses, raise test scores, and organize the data required by the law.[9]

Yet as the *Sun* noted,

> ... software claims of success tend to be based on dubious studies, often performed or paid for by the companies themselves—a problem that is acknowledged even by the Bush administration. While encouraging schools to use education technology to comply with No Child Left Behind, the administration is paying for millions of dollars in studies to determine which education software programs really work. "We're spending all this money on technology in schools and we don't know where it's effective, what the conditions are for effective teaching and learning," said Susan D. Patrick, the U.S. Department of Education's director of education technology.[10]

For every possible angle, there appears to be someone who can turn it into a market. So even as private enterprise seeks profit in test writing, test coaching, and tutoring students to do better on tests, the specter of cheating hasn't escaped entrepreneurial attention. With an eye on reports of increased fraud since the inception of NCLB and the high-stakes testing environment it has spawned, a Utah security company, Caveon, has positioned itself as the first firm to specifically provide security services in the field of K-12 high-stakes testing. The company has obtained contracts with North Carolina, South Carolina, and Delaware to audit schools' testing procedures for security strengths and weaknesses, and to recommend measures to improve security.[11]

The privatizing bias written into NCLB is only the latest development in the ongoing long-term transformation of schooling from a public good to a commodity. Public schools have always provided a number of points of entry for privatization. At the most basic level are ancillary services, such as school cafeterias, janitorial functions, or transportation programs that convey students to and from school. These programs may be contracted out to private companies rather than performed by employees hired directly by the school district itself. As long-standing and seemingly innocuous as such relationships may be, however, even they are not free of potential corruption. In Texas, journalists documented that under a newly privatized school breakfast program at Houston Independent School District, Aramark was distributing hundreds of uneaten breakfasts daily to classrooms that were then recorded as consumed—qualifying the district for $16.7 million in federal funds, with $4.75 million going back to Aramark. The school district and Aramark together are "bilking the free breakfast program for millions every year," charged Orell Fitzsimmons, leader of the union representing district food service workers and a longtime critic of the privatization program.[12]

THE EVOLVING PRIVATIZATION PARADIGM

Privatization and the forms it takes continue to evolve, branching from the management of schools into a variety of other services formerly provided by community schools and related institutions. The case of private tutoring offers just one example of the trend. NCLB requires that schools labeled as failing for three consecutive years must give parents of the children attending them access to taxpayer-funded tutoring services. Moreover, under the law, federal officials openly favor private providers over existing public schools. This was explicitly demonstrated in Chicago in 2004. Attempting to comply with the NCLB requirement for tutoring, Chicago Public Schools spent $53 million in federal funds in 2004 to provide tutoring for 80,000 students. According to the district's CEO, Arne Duncan, that's fewer than half of the number of students eligible—200,000. About 40,000 students got tutoring from private firms, at an average cost of $1,300 per student, while the other 40,000 got tutoring from district teachers, at an average cost of $400 per student. Federal education authorities, however, in late 2004 ordered the district to put all students to be tutored into private programs, claiming that since Chicago schools are "failing," they aren't qualified to provide tutoring, either.[13]

A *Chicago Tribune* editorial endorsing the federal mandate noted that one reason the district's in-house tutoring is less expensive is that tutoring groups of about 15 students are larger than the tutoring groups at private contractors. Yet even the private tutors use groups of eight to ten—two to three times what the editorial asserts is "the ideal size" for such groups.[14] In March 2005, the school district took steps to remove one agency, New York-based Platform Learning, which had a $15 million contract to tutor 14,000 children in 76 Chicago schools.[15] Duncan ejected Platform from seven of those schools, where 1,100 children were enrolled. School principals complained of chronic absenteeism among tutors and overcrowded tutoring classrooms, where children watched movies or played games because they lacked tutors. Additionally, a former Platform tutor told the *Chicago Tribune* that, contrary to a requirement that the firm develop individual tutoring plans for each child, "tutors were told to use the same plan for each child."[16] With contracts in New York, Detroit, Atlanta, Los Angeles, San Francisco, and Newark, New Jersey, Platform is one of the largest private tutoring firms to have emerged in the wake of NCLB. Its New York contract alone is reportedly worth $35 million.[17]

Even supporters of the private-tutoring mandate acknowledge, as Duncan has insisted, that there simply are not enough private contractors to fill the need.[18] That does not seem to have deterred federal regulators, who seem determined to provide the resources necessary to create an education marketplace. Federal regulators are also not deterred by the fact that large numbers of children don't appear to be getting the tutoring services for which they are eligible. In Illinois, for example, just 5.5 percent of that state's 325,944 eligible children received the mandated tutoring in 2003. Some schools failed to establish tutoring programs, while at others, parents do not appear to have enrolled their children—an outcome that led Nina Rees, assistant deputy secretary of education, to tell the *Chicago Tribune*, "Districts need to do a better job of marketing what it is they are offering."[19]

Indeed, the law does require school districts to notify parents of their eligibility for tutoring, and to contract with providers and parents for tutoring services. A 2004 survey conducted jointly by the Association of Community Organizations for Reform Now (ACORN), based in Washington, D.C., and the American Institute for Social Justice (AISJ), based in Dallas, Texas, however, found that supplemental tutoring services themselves consistently fail to be held accountable in the way that the act holds schools accountable for failing to achieve Adequate Yearly Progress (AYP).[20]

The responsibility for evaluating tutoring services themselves falls to the states, which are also assigned the job of setting AYP standards and identifying which districts must offer tutoring under the act. The ACORN/AISJ study estimated a market of $20 billion to $30 billion for various in-school services provided by private, for-profit contractors. States must evaluate supplemental service providers after two years of operation as part of the process of monitoring their performance.[21]

The ACORN/AISJ survey encompassed 91 school districts and state education departments in 29 states and the District of

Columbia. Of 24 states in which supplemental services had been offered for at least two years, "only 6, or 25 percent, had finished their evaluations of the 2003–2004 performance data," the survey found. "This means that parents are choosing providers for their children *right now* without being able to tell if the children will be getting real help with their academics."[22]

The survey found extensive problems with the evaluation process, considering it untimely and inadequate to establish the actual quality of such services, and concluded that as much as $200 million to $300 million had been spent in supplemental services in the 19 surveyed districts "with almost no scientific evidence that this spending has contributed to academic achievement."[23]

TRADE AGREEMENTS TAKE PRIVATIZATION GLOBAL

Even as private corporations, aided by state statute and federal law, insinuate themselves into the public education system domestically, the stage is being set to expand the commercialization of education around the world. This can be seen in the provisions of the trade agreements that have come to govern world trade among Western industrialized nations and that increasingly are being extended to developing countries.

The 1994 General Agreement on Trade in Services (GATS) and earlier international trade agreements have begun to create a framework that views education as "a commodity rather than consciousness-raising experience," according to Reaves. He adds, "In doing so, schools are transformed from a public good to private privilege, from a social service to potentials for profit."[24] Reaves argues that globalization and privatization, rather than being either inevitable or even desirable, "are carefully orchestrated initiatives put forward by governmental leaders, business executives, and international financial institutions to reshape societies and create economic environments that ensure profits for corporations." Among the engines that power both forces are international trade agreements, negotiated by governments for the express purpose of creating favorable environments for corporations.

In framing a global marketplace, GATS, for example, treats education not as a public trust but as a profit opportunity. It thus encourages the development of phenomena such as the "World Education Market" held in May 2000 under the sponsorship of Paris-based Reed Midem. That event boasted 3,000 participants, 100 speakers, and 458 exhibits. The conference described the "education business" as a new "industry" with a "global market," and encouraged interest on the part of "investors."[25] A subsequent conference was held in 2003 in Lisbon, Portugal (www.wemex.com).

The World Education Market assumes learning and the educative process to be simply one more bundle of commodities, ripe for globalization and profit maximizers;[26] indeed, a Merrill Lynch analyst valued the "international education marketplace" at $2 trillion annually, or 5 percent of global GDP.[27]

Article I, Section 3(b) of GATS specifically exempts foreign-based competition for "services provided to the public in the exercise of governmental authority."[28] Education, however, does not appear to fall under that umbrella; instead of being identified as a government-provided public service, it has become a "knowledge industry"—a business rather than a social service.[29] A critical assessment of the agreement suggests that the ambiguous definitions of governmental services and scope of regulations in GATS point the way toward "forcing governments to treat their own public services, such as education and health, on the same basis as privately run services."[30]

Following the logic inherent in the agreement's treatment of education, Rikowski observes that "every time the private sector enters, deepens, and expands its involvement in our schools, it opens those 'educational services' to the GATS."[31] The very logical prospect, he tells his British audience, is that in due time, "a company in Detroit or Vancouver that focuses primarily on the bottom line could control your local secondary school"[32]—in the process defying the conventional understanding of democratically accountable community schools.

THE TRIUMPH OF IMAGE OVER SUBSTANCE

The spread of commercialism throughout American culture, including its reach into public education, has not taken place without sharp critiques, by writers such as Susan Linn, Alissa Quart, Naomi Klein, and Juliet Schor, and by activist groups such as Commercial Alert. Founded in 1998 by Ralph Nader and Gary Ruskin, Commercial Alert (www.commercialalert.org) takes as its mission "to keep the commercial culture within its proper sphere, and to prevent it from exploiting children and subverting the higher values of family, community, environmental integrity, and democracy." The organization issues statements criticizing developments in commercial encroachment of public space and institutions and seeks to organize grassroots activists to oppose such developments.

Adbusters, both a magazine based in Vancouver, B.C., Canada, and an international activist collective (The Adbusters Media Foundation), offers pointed criticism and subversion of mainstream media and advertising/marketing practices. The organization (at www.adbusters.org) founded by Kalle Lasn, a documentarist, launched and promotes "Buy Nothing Day" (the day after the American Thanksgiving holiday—traditionally the start of the Christmas shopping season in the United States) and "TV Turnoff Week" (generally the last week in April). Adbusters is particularly noteworthy for its studied use of irony and the skills of the organization's activists to perform a sort of antimarketing jujitsu.

The voices of such critics, however, are often lost in the contemporary marketing-dominated social, political, and economic environment. The ascendance of marketing coincides with the transformation of the American economy, and the world's, from agrarian to industrial to post-industrial, based on the exchange of "services." An economy that once revolved around making and exchanging tangible things now revolves around trade in intangible services. American companies increasingly focus on building brands—images—while contracting out the manufacturing to others, often located overseas in low-wage havens such as China, India, and Southeast Asia. The significance of a product has come to reside less in its three-dimensional attributes than in the place it occupies in the mind of the consumer.

Along with our virtual economy, we have developed a sort of virtual politics. Modern political campaigns are not about the crafting and presentation of specific ideas about how to run complex governmental institutions or how to meet the varied and sometimes conflicting needs of a diverse population. Instead, political campaigns have devolved into competing advertising campaigns that market candidates as products. To a considerable degree, reality no longer matters in the American political process. Image is all. To turn an old advertising aphorism on its head, steak no longer matters—only the sizzle. Modern American political campaigns provide clear evidence of the extent to which market values have displaced civic culture.

In *Experience and Education*, John Dewey describes an educative experience as being part of a continuity of experiences that promote individual and community growth. Continuity of experience is, as he saw it, necessary both to provide context and meaning to immediate experiences and to shape subsequent experiences in the service of individual purposes. In his words, "No experience is educative that does not tend both to knowledge of more facts and entertaining of more ideas and to a better, a more orderly, arrangement of them."[33] Where Dewey seeks the integrative experiences in the service of the individual and the community, advertising destroys continuity, fragments experience, and encourages us to act on irrational impulses for the purpose of manipulating our behavior.

The twentieth century saw increasingly powerful efforts to transform the ideal of public schools as democratizing civic institutions into the ideal of schools as a consumer marketplace. The education marketplace is intended to provide inviting venues for advertising and public relations, and to offer up schools themselves as commodities to be bought and sold. To succeed, efforts to create an education marketplace must necessarily seek to remove control of schools from the communities they serve. Thus, market-oriented measures to reform schools don't reflect popular will so much as they reflect the ideological supremacy of economic efficiency over all other values in elite political decision making and the abandonment of democratic values in favor of a social order tied together by the values of the marketplace.

Market values are concerned with buying and selling. They offer no guidance on matters of justice or fairness, and cannot, therefore, represent the interests of all children. Turning children over to the market ensures that they inevitably will be treated as an expense to be reduced or a resource to be harvested. In the process, some children and their families necessarily will be considered more valuable than others. For the market to produce winners, it requires that there be losers. While all societies produce losers, this may be the first time a society has explicitly sought to do so.

NOTES

NOTES TO INTRODUCTION

1. R. Arnove and C. A. Torres, eds, *Comparative Education: The Dialectics of the Global and the Local* (Lanham, MD.: Rowman and Littlefield, 1999, second edition, 2003).

2. A detailed analysis of the contemporary trends in educational reform impacted by globalization and neoliberalism, with an emphasis on the discourse during the recent presidential campaigns, can be found in the my article "NCLB: A Brainchild of Neoliberalism and American Politics" in *New Politics* 8 (winter 2005) (see www.newpol.org).

3. Carlos Alberto Torres, "Expert Knowledge, External Assistance, and Educational Reform in the Age of Neoliberalism: A Focus on the World Bank and Question of Moral Responsibilities in Third World Educational Reform," in Marilyn Gittell, Bernd Reiter, and Michael Sharpe, eds., *Old and New Frontiers in Education Reform: Confronting Exclusion in the Democratic Tradition* (New York, Lexington Books, in press).

4. Robert Rhoads and Carlos Alberto Torres, eds., *States, Markets, and Higher Education: The Political Economy of Higher Education in the Americas* (Stanford CA: Stanford University Press, in press).

NOTES TO CHAPTER 1

1. John DeGraaf, David Wann, Thomas H. Naylor, *Affluenza: The All-Consuming Epidemic* (San Francisco: Berrett-Koehler Publishers, 2002).

2. Lesley Brown, ed., *The New Shorter Oxford English Dictionary* (Oxford, UK: Clarendon Press, 1993) 451.

3. James B. Twitchell, *Lead Us into Temptation* (New York: Columbia University Press, 1999) 30.

4. Michael F. Jacobson and Laurie Ann Mazur, *Marketing Madness* (Boulder, CO: Westview Press, 1995) 12.

5. Juliet B. Schor, *The Overspent American* (New York: Basic Books, 1998).

6. Thomas Frank, *The Conquest of Cool* (Chicago: University of Chicago Press, 1997).

7. Naomi Klein, *No Logo* (New York: Picador, 2000, 2002).

8. Eric Schlosser, *Fast Food Nation* (New York: Houghton & Mifflin, 2001).

9. Susan Linn, *Consuming Kids: The Hostile Takeover of Childhood* (New York: The New Press, 2004).

10. Alissa, Quart *Branded: The Buying and Selling of Teenagers* (Cambridge, UK: Perseus Books, 2003).

11. Juliet Schor, *Born to Buy: The Commercialized Child and the New Consumer Culture* (New York: Scribner, 2004) 13.

12. Schor, *Born to Buy*, 20.

13. Schor, *Born to Buy*, 21.

14. Vivica Kraak and David L. Pelletier, "The Influence of Commercialism on the Food Purchasing Behavior of Children and Teenage Youth," *Family Economics and Nutrition Review* 11, no. 3 (1998), 15–24.

15. Campaign for a Commercial-Free Childhood. *The Facts About Marketing to Kids*. Available: http://www.commercialexploitation.org/factsheets/entirebooklet.pdf.

16. *The Facts About Marketing to Kids*.

17. James U. McNeal, *Kids as Customers: A Handbook of Marketing to Children* (New York: Lexington Books, 1992).

18. E. Broome, Report of the Committee on Propaganda in the Schools. Presented at the Atlanta meeting of the National Education Association, July 1929.

19. Broome, Report of the Committee on Propaganda in the Schools.

20. McNeal, *Kids as Customers*.

21. Schor, *Born to Buy*, 174.
22. National Commission on Excellence in Education. *A Nation at Risk: The Imperatives for Educational Reform*. Washington, DC: U.S. Department of Education, 1983.
23. A. Molnar, D. Garcia, J. Joanu, C. Sullivan, B. McEvoy, & E. Griffin, Profiles of For-Profit Education Management Companies: Seventh-Annual Report 2004–2005. Tempe, AZ: Education Policy Studies Laboratory, Education Policy Research Unit and Commercialism in Education Research Unit, March 2005 [online]. Available: http://www.asu.edu/educ/epsl/CERU/Documents/EPSL-0503-101-CERU.pdf.

NOTES TO CHAPTER 2

1. Alex Molnar, *Sponsored Schools and Commercialized Classrooms: Schoolhouse Commercializing Trends in the 1990s*, Milwaukee: University of Wisconsin–Milwaukee, Center for the Analysis of Commercialism in Education, August 1998, 1–6.
2. Chris Berdik, "Your All-Mall Mater," *Boston Globe*, May 30, 2004, D2.
3. David Barboza, "If You Pitch It, They Will Eat," *New York Times*, Section 3, Aug. 3, 2003, 1.
4. Alex Molnar, *Virtually Everywhere: Marketing to Children in America's Schools: The Seventh Annual Report on Trends in Schoolhouse Commercialism, Year 2003–2004* (Tempe, AZ: Arizona State University, Education Policy Studies Laboratory, Commercialism in Education Research Unit, 2004).
5. Molnar, *Virtually Everywhere*.
6. Matthew Klein, "School Daze," *Marketing Tools*, September 1997, 16.
7. E. Broome, Report of the Committee on Propaganda in the Schools. Presented at the Atlanta meeting of the National Education Association, July 1929.
8. Association for Supervision and Curriculum Development Liaison Committee on Instructional Materials, *Using Free Materials in the Classroom* (Washington, DC: Association for Supervision and Curriculum Development), 1953.
9. American Association of School Administrators, *Choosing Free Materials for Use in the Schools* (Washington, DC: American Association of School Administrators), 1955.

10. Sheila Harty, *Hucksters in the Classroom: A Review of Industry Propaganda in Schools* (Washington, DC: Center for Study of Responsive Law), 1979.

11. Harty, *Hucksters in the Classroom*.

12. Consumers Union, *Captive Kids: Commercial Pressures on Kids at School* (Yonkers, NY: Consumers Union Education Services, 1995), 12–16.

13. Roy F. Fox, "Manipulated Kids: Teens Tell How Ads Influence Them," *Educational Leadership*, 53, no. 1 (September 1995): 77–79; and Roy F. Fox, "Flavor Crystals as Brain Food: Unplug TV Commercials in School," *Phi Delta Kappan* 79, no. 4 (December 1997): 326–327.

14. Mark Crispin Miller, *How to Be Stupid: The Teachings of Channel One* (Alexandria, VA: Association for Supervision and Curriculum Development, 1997) ERIC Document Reproduction Service, no. ED428460.

15. Hugh Rank, "Channel One/Misconceptions Three," *English Journal* 81, no. 4 (April 1992): 31–32; and Hugh Rank, "Channel One: Asking the Wrong Questions," *Educational Leadership*, 51, no. 4 (December 1993–January 1994): 52–55.

16. M. Morgan, Channel One in the Public Schools: Widening the Gaps. (Oakland, CA: UNPLUG, 1993), ERIC Document Reproduction Service, no. ED366688.

17. B. S. Greenberg and J. E. Brand, "Channel One: But What About the Advertising?" *Educational Leadership* 51: 56–58.

18. Roy Fox, "Manipulated Kids," *Stay Free* 13 (1997); reprinted from *Educational Leadership*, September 1995.

19. Susan A. Smith, "Program Gets Blurry Reception," *The News-Leader* (Springfield, MO), Nov. 15, 2003, online at www.news-leader.com/today/1115-Programget-216980.html (retrieved Dec. 4, 2003).

20. "Council Led by Former U.S. Education Secretaries Provides Guidelines for Model School Business Relationships," press release distributed by PR Newswire for the Council for Corporate and School Partnerships, Sept. 25, 2002.

21. "Council led by former U.S. education secretaries," press release.

22. "Council led by former U.S. education secretaries," press release.

23. Chris Berdik, "Your All-Mall Mater," *Boston Globe*, May 30, 2004, D2.

24. Berdik, "Your All-Mall Mater."

25. Berdik, "Your All-Mall Mater."

26. Analyses conducted in 1998, 1999, and 2000 were undertaken by CACE. Those conducted in 2001, 2002, 2003 and 2004 were

conducted by CERU. For simplification, all subsequent references will refer to these reports as CERU's research.

27. "Sports Briefs," *Florida Times-Union* (Jacksonville), Aug. 13, 2003, M7.

Leila Cobo, "McTour for Latin rock," *Billboard*, Aug, 9, 2003, 49.

28. Robert Ruth, "Youngsters' Gadgets Tackle Problems of Everyday Living," *Columbus Dispatch*, May 23, 2004, 8C.

29. "People," *News and Observer* (Raleigh, NC), Aug. 27, 2003, B7.

30. Sue Ter Maat, "Streamwood High Student Wins Award," *Chicago Daily Herald*, Neighbor, May 14, 2004, 1.

31. Logan Mabe, "Pepsi High," *St. Petersburg Times*, Aug. 31, 2003, 1D.

32. Ken Dixon, "Stem-Cell Research, Business Tax Among Dozens of Bills Killed," *Connecticut Post* (Bridgeport, CT), May 6, 2004.

33. Michele Miller, "Judging a Book by the Costume," *St. Petersburg Times/Pasco Times*, Oct. 8, 2003, 3.

"Schools across America Celebrate National Young Readers Day," press release for Pizza Hut distributed by PR Newswire, Nov. 5, 2003.

34. "Local Leader Receives National Honor for Lifelong Commitment to Supporting His Community," press release for McDonald's Corp. distributed by PR Newswire, Nov. 6, 2003.

35. Barri Bronston, "Summertime Is Story Time," *Times-Picayune* (New Orleans, LA), Living, May 31, 2004, 1.

36. "School News," *Times-Picayune*, (New Orleans, LA), March 14, 2004, 8.

37. Meredith Amdur, "Marvel Deal Set to Cover Schoolkids," *Daily Variety*, Dec. 19, 2003, 8.

38. "Lee County Schools Consider Selling Naming Rights, Bus Ads," Associated Press, Aug. 14, 2003.

39. Jeffrey White, "School Bus Ads an 'Excellent Idea,'" *Patriot Ledger* (Quincy, MA), Oct. 27, 2003, 1.

Tamara Race, " Ads on School Buses OK'd," *Patriot Ledger* (Quincy, MA), April 27, 2004, 10.

40. Aimee Green, "District Decides Background Checks Policy," *The Oregonian* (Portland, OR), Dec. 11, 2003, C2.

41. Andea Eger, "Commercials in Buses Could 'Ad' up Quickly," *Tulsa World*, Oct. 12, 2003, A1.

42. "Miami-Dade County Schools Consider Selling Ads to Be Placed Inside Buses," *Miami Herald*, distributed by Knight Ridder/ Tribune Business News, Aug. 19, 2003.

43. Carrie MacMillan, "Readin,' Writin,' and Sellin,'" *Promo,* Sept. 1, 2002.

44. Goeff Mulvihill, "Name This School—Sponsors Helping District's Cash Flow," Associated Press, reprinted in *The Commercial Appeal* (Memphis, TN), April 19, 2004, A4.

45. Quoted in Olivia Freeman, "What Next—Product Placement in the Classroom?" *Irish Times*, May 27, 2004, 18.

46. Olivia Freeman, "What Next?"

47. John Chavez, "Movie *Elf* to Feature Ohio Toy Maker's Etch-a-Sketch," *Toledo Blade*, Nov. 8, 2003.

48. Steve Harrison, "Big Business Teaches Some Lessons to Miami-Area Elementary-School Students," *Miami Herald*, distributed by Knight Ridder/Tribune Business News, Jan. 12, 2004.

49. Kathleen Joyce, "Celebrating the Best," *Promo*, Nov. 1, 2003, 11.

50. "Dear Educator...," *Current Health* 2, a *Weekly Reader* publication 5, no. 30, Jan. 1, 2004.

51. "Dear Educator..."

52. "McDonald's Unveils Bold Balanced Lifestyles Platform," press release distributed for McDonald's by PR Newswire, April 15, 2004.

53. Debra Kaufman, "Channel One Outlasts Its Critics; In-School Commercials Remain a Sore Point for Opposition," *Television Week*, Nov. 24, 2003, 18.

    "The History Channel and Comcast Partner with the School District of Philadelphia," press release for The History Channel distributed by PR Newswire, Dec. 28, 2003.

54. M.C. Antil, "TWC, Greenberg Making a Difference," *Cablefax* 14, no. 165 (Aug. 26, 2003).

55. Evan Hansen, "Public Schools: Why Johnny Can't Blog," CNET News.com, Nov. 13, 2003, online at http://news.com/2009-1023-5103805.html (retrieved Dec. 4, 2003).

    Mensah M. Dean, "District, Microsoft partners in new $46M high school," *Philadelphia Daily News*, Sept. 5, 2003, online at www.philly.com/mld/philly/news/local/6696550.htm (retrieved March 7, 2005).

56. Richard Turcsik, "Sweet Charity," *Progressive Grocer*, Oct. 1, 2003.

    Jennifer Arend, "School Cashes in on Shopper's Win; Box Tops Program Generating Extra Income for Campuses," *The Dallas Morning News*, May 6, 2004, 1Y.

57. Marianne D. Hurst, "Parent Poll: Schools Using Fund-Raising for Basics," *Education Week*, Jan. 21, 2004.

58. Hurst, "Parent Poll."

59. Omar Sacirbey, "To Pay Bills, Schools in Europe Allow Ads," *Christian Science Monitor*, March 19, 1999, 1.

60. Pete Lewis, "Corporate Sponsors Help with Financing; Funding for Denver, Colorado Public Schools," *Denver Business Journal*, Nov. 20, 1998, 6B.

61. Helen Jones, "Brands Enter the Classroom," *Financial Times* (London), September 1, 1997, 13.

62. "Campbell's: History, 1970's" (chronology), online at http://campbellsoup.com/center/history/1970.html. (retrieved July 26, 1999).

63. Campbell's corporate press release, "On Your Mark! Get Set! Go!," Canada NewsWire, June 24, 1999.

64. Ruth Walker, "Canada Tunes In to TV—and Ads—in the Classroom," *Christian Science Monitor*, June 22, 1999, 14.

65. Ontario Secondary School Teacher's Federation, "Commercialization in Our Schools," AMPA 2001 House Paper, online at www.osstf.on.ca/www/abosstf/ampa01/commercialization/positivetrends.html (retrieved March 7, 2005).

66. Sarah Gault, "Principals See Merit in Ad Plan," *Daily News* (New Plymouth, New Zealand), June 18, 1999, 1.

67. Gault, "Principals See Merit."

68. Leanne Dohy, "Schools May Bear Business Names," *Calgary Herald*, Dec. 6, 2003, A1; "Sponsoring Schools," *The Nelson Mail*, Dec. 23, 2003, 13.

69. Chelsea Jones, "'Bribing' Students into Fund-raising," *The Leader-Post* (Regina, Saskatchewan), Dec. 15, 2003, B8.

70. "More Choice for Schools," *Ottawa Citizen*, Dec. 1, 2003, B4.

71. See, for example,

  National Commission on Excellence in Education, *A Nation at Risk: The Imperative for Educational Reform*, Washington, DC: Author, 1983.

  CEO Forum on Education and Technology, "Professional Development: A Link to Better Learning," Washington, DC: Author, 1999.

  Achieve, Inc., *National Education Summit Briefing Book*, Washington, DC: Author, 1999.

72. Erika Rasmusson, "Courting the Classroom: Advertising in Schools," *Sales & Marketing Management*, September 1997, 20.

73. Pete Lewis, "Corporate Sponsors Help with Financing; Funding for Denver, Colorado Public Schools," *Denver Business Journal*, Nov. 20, 1998, 6B.

74. AP, "Cash-Strapped Schools Turn to Marketing Deals," Cable News Network Web site, Jan. 15, 2004, online at www.cnn.com/2004/EDUCATION/01/15/schools.commercialism.ap/index.html (retrieved July 13, 2004).

75. AP, "Cash-Strapped Schools."

76. Curt Seeden, "Parents' Goal: Save Class-Size Reduction," *The Orange County Register* (California), Nov. 27, 2003.

77. Tim Hay, "Sponsored Classes," *San Mateo County Times*, Aug. 16, 2003.

78. Michael P. McKinney, "Fees to Ride School Buses Will Drive Revenue Efforts in Seekonk, Mass.," *Providence Journal*, distributed by Knight Ridder/Tribune Business News, 2003, July 29, 2003.

79. Steven Rosenberg, "Tight Budget Could Prompt School Closing," *Boston Globe*, March 18, 2004, 1; and Alex Lyda, "Parents Try to save Elementary School from the Budget Ax," *San Diego Union-Tribune*, March 21, 2004, B2.

80. "Citizens, School Board Members in West Bend Struggle to Cut Budget," *Milwaukee Journal Sentinel* (Wisconsin), July 24, 2003, 1B.

81. Karen Nugent, "Nashoba Raises Fees for Student Athletes," *Telegram & Gazette* (Worcester, MA), July 24, 2003, B1.

82. Alex Johnson, "A Crash Course in Raw Economics; Schools Dream up New Ways to Pay the Bills," MSNBC News/*Newsweek* Aug. 25, 2003, online at http://msnbc.msn.com/id/3070983 (retrieved July 19, 2004).

83. Jim Szymanski, "Schools Look at New Tools for Raising Dollars," *News Tribune* (Tacoma, WA), Aug. 25, 2003, B1.

84. Szymanski, "Schools Look at New Tools."

85. Rhea Borja, "Districts Use eBay to Sell Old School Buildings, Desks," *Education Week*, Oct. 1, 2003.

86. Debra Nussbaum, "Adding a Little Extra to the Education Pot," *New York Times*, section 14NJ, May 2, 2004, 6.

87. Raymond Kelly, "Punishment Undeserved," *Fort Pierce Tribune*, March 21, 2003, A10.

88. Stephanie Dunnewind, "Beyond Bake Sales," *Seattle Times*, Aug. 31, 2003, E1.

89. Bonnie Miller Rubin, "Reading, Writing, Retailing? Schools' Field Trips Increasingly Flock to Stores," *Chicago Tribune*, distributed by Knight Ridder/Tribune Business News, Feb. 23, 2004.

90. Carlos Frias and David A. Markiewicz, "Searching for a Star: Major Companies Latch on to Top High School Athletes by Offering Free

Shoes and Equipment for Their Teams," *Atlanta Journal-Constitution*, March 7, 2004, 1A.

91. Frias and Markiewicz, "Searching for a Star."

92. Frias and Markiewicz, "Searching for a Star."

93. Center for the Study of Commercialism, "Get the Message? Growing Up in a Commercial Culture," in *Living in a Material World: Lessons on Commercialism, Consumption, and Environment*, Washington, D.C.: Author, 1996; distributed by the Center for Science in the Public Interest, Washington, DC.

94. Dina Bunn, "Teen Spenders Wield Great Power," *Rocky Mountain News*, Nov. 15 1998, 4G.

95. Leslie Baldacci, "Study Reveals Surprises about Teen Eating Habits," *Sun-Times*, October 7, 1998, 1.

96. Dan Carden, "Schools Find Soft Drink Cash Refreshing," *Pantagraph* (Bloomington, IL), July 19, 1998, A3.

97. Caroline E. Mayer, "Nurturing Brand Loyalty; with Preschool Supplies, Firms Woo Future Customers—and Current Parents" *Washington Post*, Oct. 12, 2003, F1.

98. "A Unique Experience in Marketing Education," *Techniques*, 78, no. 7 (Oct. 2003): 22–26, 42.

99. Rhea Borja, "Schools Banking on Financial-Literacy Efforts," *Education Week*, April 28, 2004.

100. Borja, "Schools Banking."

101. Bruce Mohl, "Commercial Break: A Company Profits from Taking Kids on Field Trips to Retail Outlets, but What Are They Learning?" *The Boston Globe*, Business, April 4, 2004, 1.

102. Edward Lee Pitts, "Stores Open Doors to Field Trips," *Chattanooga Times Free Press,* July 21, 2003, B1.

103. Mohl, "Commercial Break."

104. Mohl, "Commercial Break."

105. "Reading, Writing and Shopping," *Buffalo News*, April 26, 2004, A7.

106. Carol Angrisani, "H-E-Buddy Children's Program Grows Up," *Supermarket News*, Feb. 9, 2004, 53.

107. Miller Rubin, "Reading, Writing, Retailing?"

108. "Brand-Name Field Trips—A Total Sellout," *Philadelphia Inquirer*, May 29, 2004, distributed by Knight Ridder/Tribune News Service.

109. Sean Alfano, "School Lessons at the Local Store; As Budgets Shrink, Schools Try Company-Sponsored Field Trips," MSNBC/*Newsweek*, Aug. 28. 2003, online at http://msnbc.msn.com/id/3070974 (retrieved July 19, 2004).

110. Alfano, "School Lessons at the Local Store."

111. Alfano, "School Lessons at the Local Store."

112. Joseph Moylan, "On Target for Alternative Education," *Principal Leadership*, 4, no. 4 (Dec. 2003): 54–57.

113. Moylan, "On Target."

114. Barbara Powell, "Growing Importance of Image Drives up Automakers' Philanthropy," Associated Press/*Commercial Appeal* (Memphis), Aug. 31, 2003, G1.

115. Powell, "Growing Importance of Image."

116. Melanie Shortman, "Artful Communication," *PR Week*, Jan. 12, 2004, 21.

117. "Female Athletes Celebrated in Acclaimed Photo Exhibition," press release distributed for MassMutual Financial Group by PR Newswire, March 26, 2004.

118. Chick-fil-A Web site, "Company and Opportunities," online at www.chickfila.com/Company.asp (retrieved July 22, 2004).

119. "Chick-fil-A and PBS' Between the Lions Announce Two-Year Sponsorship," press release distributed for Chick-fil-A by PR Newswire, Jan. 21, 2004.

120. "Audubon Society Donates Nature Education Kits," *Post-Standard* (Syracuse, NY), July 17, 2003, 20.

121. Ron Harris, "Hollywood Takes Its Fight with Piracy into Schools," The Associated Press, reprinted in the *Deseret News* (Salt Lake City, UT), Oct. 31, 2003, W8.

122. Harris, "Hollywood Takes Its Fight."

123. Steve Harrison, "Big Business Teaches Some Lessons to Miami-Area Elementary-School Students," *Miami Herald*, distributed by Knight Ridder/Tribune Business News, Jan. 12, 2004.

124. Chuck McCollough, "Bus Ad Bucks Not Growing," *San Antonio Express-News*, January 27, 1999, 1H.

125. Telephone communication with Chuck Phipps, director of enrollment and audit for Colorado Springs School District 11, July 26, 1999.

126. Erin Emery, "Colorado Springs Schools Face Cuts to Budget; District 11 Proposes Slicing $4.8 Million," *Denver Post*, March 16, 1999, B04.

127. KA Graham, "Brooklawn, N.J., School Gym Takes on ShopRite Name after Receiving $100,000," *The Philadelphia Inquirer*, Nov. 16, 2001.

128. D. Russakoff, "Finding the Wrongs in Naming Rights; School Gym Sponsorship Sparks Furor," *Washington Post*, Dec. 16, 2001, A3.

129. David Slade, "District Considers TV Deal," *Morning Call* (Allentown, PA), Nov. 12, 2003, B1.

130. Josh Buice, "One Channel Worth Changing," *Atlanta Journal-Constitution*, July 31, 2003, 23A.

131. Cara DeGette, "To Ensure Revenue, Coke Is It; Schools Urged to Boost Sales," *Denver Post*, Nov. 22 1998, B1.

132. John Bushey, "District 11's Coke Problem," *Harper's*, February 1999.

133. Marc Kaufman, "Pop Culture: Health Advocates Sound Alarm as Schools Strike Deals with Coke and Pepsi," *Washington Post*, March 23, 1999, Z12.

134. Constance L. Hays, "Today's Lesson: Soda Rights; Consultant Helps Schools Sell Themselves to Vendors," *New York Times*, May 21, 1999, C1.

135. Kaufman, "Pop Culture."

136. Hayes, "Today's Lesson."

137. Matthew Kauffman, "True or False? Ads Go off Limits," *Hartford Courant*, Nov. 5, 2003, E1.

138. Angie Welling, "There Oughta Be a Law, Judge Says," *Deseret Morning News* (Salt Lake City), July 31, 2003, B1.

139. "State Has a Right to Keep Schools Peaceful." *Deseret Morning News* (Salt Lake City), Aug. 3, 2003, AA1.

140. Berdik, "Your All-Mall Mater."

141. Rhea Borja, "Cash-Strapped Oregon Schools Get Help from Businesses," *Education Week*, Nov. 19, 2003.

142. William Yelverton, "Financial Pinches in Schools Call for Creative Thinking," *Tampa Tribune*, Pasco section, Aug. 17, 2003, B2.

143. "Dignity vs. Dough," *Arkansas Democrat-Gazette*, Aug. 6, 2003, 18.

144. "Dignity vs. Dough," *Arkansas Democrat-Gazette*.

145. Jay T. Engeln, "Capitol Hill Hearing Testimony," Federal Document Clearing House, March 30, 2004.

146. Bob Geiger, "Minneapolis Marketing Briefs," *Finance & Commerce* (Minneapolis), distributed by Dolan Media Newswires, April 17, 2004.

147. Geiger, "Minneapolis Marketing Briefs."

148. D. Riesman, N. Glazer, and R. Denney, *The Lonely Crowd: A Study of the Changing American Character*, rev. ed. (Garden City, NY: Doubleday and Co., Inc., 1955).

149. V. Packard, *The Hidden Persuaders* (New York: Pocket Books, Inc.), 1957.

150. S. Jhally, *Advertising and the End of the World* (video) (Amherst, MA: Media Education Foundation video, 1998); and S. Jhally, *The Codes of Advertising: Fetishism and the Political Economy of Meaning in the Consumer Society* (New York: St. Martin's Press; London: Frances Pinter, 1987).

NOTES TO CHAPTER 3

1. W. M. Payne, "Mini McDonald's Opens at Fleming Elementary," *Michigan Chronicle*, Dec. 7, 1999, B3.
2. Janet K. Bunton, e-mail personal communication, Sept. 27, 2004.
3. Consumers Union, *Captive Kids: Commercial Pressures on Kids at School*, Yonkers, NY: Consumers Union Education Services, 1995.
4. Pathways Group, Inc., corporate press release, "Pathways to Bring Smart Card Technology to Hawaii High School Students," May 28, 1999.
5. Allison Bruce, "Charleston Schools Go Pepsi Only," *Post and Courier* (Charleston, SC), Aug. 9, 2002, 1A.
6. Logan Mabe, "Pepsi High," *St. Petersburg Times,* Aug. 31, 2003, 1D.
7. Carolyn Bower, "Soda Machines in Schools Are Big Business," *St. Louis Post-Dispatch* Aug. 29, 2003 A1.
8. Bower, "Soda Machines in Schools."
9. Brian McTaggart, "Selling Our Schools: Districts Cashing in on Deals with Soft Drink Firms," *Houston Chronicle,* Aug. 10, 1997, A1, Two Star Edition.
10. "Tarrant County, Texas, Cities Try to Pinch Pennies in Annual Budgets," *Fort Worth Star-Telegram,* distributed by Knight Ridder/Tribune Business News, July 21, 2003.
11. See, for example, "How to Make Reading a Family Activity This Summer," press release distributed by PR Newswire for Pizza Hut, July 9, 2001.

    "Kids Get Wild about Reading with Pizza and Lions," press release distributed by PR Newswire for Pizza Hut, Nov. 10, 2001.
12. Business briefs column, *Florida Keyes Keynoter,* distributed by Knight Ridder/Tribune Business News, Aug. 27, 2003.
13. Fact Sheet: Foods and Beverages Sold Outside of School Meal Programs. *Centers for Disease Control School Health Policies and Programs Study (SHPPS)*; 2002. Online at: www.cdc.gov/HealthyYouth/shpps/factsheets/foods_sold_outside_school.htm (retrieved March 4, 2005).
14. Richard Turcsik, "Sweet Charity," *Progressive Grocer,* Oct. 1, 2003.
15. Turcsik, "Sweet Charity."

    Jennifer Arend, "School Cashes in on Shopper's Win; Box Tops Program Generating Extra Income for Campuses," *The Dallas Morning News,* May 6, 2004, 1Y.
16. "Parents Club News," *The Times-Picayune* (New Orleans), Metairie Picayune section, Sept. 29, 2002, 5.

17. "General Mills Supports Struggling Schools with Box Tops for Education," press release distributed by Internet Wire for General Mills, Sept. 25, 2002.

18. "Education: School Fund-Raisers," *Newsweek*, Oct. 7, 2002, 73.

19. "Education: School Fund-Raisers," *Newsweek*.

20. "Teachers and Principals Work behind McDonald's Counter to Raise Funds for Education," press release distributed by PR Newswire for McDonald's, Oct. 17, 2002.

21. "McDonald's and Local Schools Raise Money in Sixteen Western States," press release distributed by PR Newswire for McDonald's, Oct. 18, 2002.

22. Paul King, "On-Sight Insight: Corporate Sponsorships Can Serve a Valuable Purpose," *Nation's Restaurant News*, April 14, 1997, 16.

23. Carrie MacMillan, "Readin,' Writin,' and Sellin,'" *Promo*, Sept. 1, 2002.

24. MacMillan, "Readin,' Writin,' and Sellin.'"

25. Michael Applebaum, "Don't Spare the Brand," *Brandweek*, March 10, 2003.

26. "When Chips Are Down, Nabisco Offers Lesson That Kids Eat Up," *Selling to Kids*, Oct. 15, 1997.

27. Kate Fitzgerald, "Mars' Twix Gives Schoolkids a Vote on How to Conclude Ad," *Advertising Age*, September 29, 1997, 48.

28. S. Thompson, "Cadbury's Candy Push," *Advertising Age*, Dec. 3, 2001, 8.

29. Caroline Grannan, "Industry Claims Kids Don't Drink Much Soda," Press release distributed by Parents Advocating School Accountability, May 12, 2003 (quoting the *Atlanta Journal-Constitution*, April 6, 2003).

30. Damien Cristodero, "Schools Find Aid in Ads, Sponsorships," *St. Petersburg Times*, South Pinellas Edition, Sports sec., January 20, 1998, 1C.

31. Jo Ann Zuniga, "School Vending Machines Criticized," *Houston Chronicle*, Aug. 28, 2003, A34.

32. Seanna Adcox, "School Drink Machines at Center of Health Debate," *Post and Courier*, July 6, 2004, A1. online at http://archives.postand-courier.com/archive/arch04/0704/arc07061810374.shtml (retrieved March 8, 2005).

33. Marc Kaufman, "Pop Culture: Health Advocates Sound Alarm as Schools Strike Deals with Coke and Pepsi," *Washington Post*, March 23, 1999, Z12.

34. M. F. Jacobson, "Liquid Candy: How Soft Drinks Are Harming Americans' Health," 1998, online at www.cspinet.org/sodapop/liquid_candy.htm (retrieved March 8, 2005).

35. E. Nagourney, "Cola Is No Boon for Bones, Study Says," *New York Times,* June 20, 2000, D8.

    G. Wyshak, "Teenaged Girls, Carbonated Beverage Consumption, and Bone Fractures," *Archives of Pediatrics and Adolescent Medicine,* 154, No. 6, June 2000, 610–613, online at http://archpedi.ama-assn.org/cgi/content/full/154/6/610 (subscription or purchase only).

36. Marc Kaufman, "Pop Culture: Health Advocates Sound Alarm as Schools Strike Deals with Coke and Pepsi," *Washington Post,* March 23, 1999, Z12.

37. Kaufman, "Pop Culture."

38. "Obesity on the Rise, New Data Show," *National Center for Health Statistics,* Press Release, Oct. 8, 2002, online at www.cdc.gov/nchs/pressroom/02news/obesityonrise.htm (retrieved March 8, 2005).

39. G. Tirozzi, "Challenges Facing Our Schools," speech delivered at the White House Healthy Schools Summit, Washington, DC, Oct. 7, 2002.

40. "The Health Risks of Obesity," *RAND Health,* March 22, 2002, online at www.rand.org/congress/health/0602/obesity/rb4549 (retrieved March 8, 2005).

41. Matthias B. Schulze, et al., "Sugar-Sweetened Beverages, Weight Gain, and Incidence of Type 2 Diabetes in Young and Middle-Aged Women," *Journal of the American Medical Association* 292 (Aug. 25, 2004): 927–34.

42. Jeffrey P. Koplan, Catharyn T. Liverman, and Vivica A. Kraak, eds., *Preventing Childhood Obesity: Health in the Balance* (Washington, DC, National Institute of Medicine, Committee on Prevention of Obesity in Children and Youth, 2005).

    David Kiley, "A Food Fight over Obesity in Kids," *Business Week,* Sept. 30, 2004, online at www.businessweek.com/bwdaily/dnflash/sep2004/nf20040930_0110_db035.htm (retrieved March 8, 2005).

43. Caroline E. Mayer, McDonald's makes Ronald a health ambassador. *Washington Post,* Jan. 28, 2005, E1. Online at http://www.washingtonpost.com/wp-dyn/articles/A43011-2005Jan27.html (retrieved March 3, 2005).

44. Associated Press, "Schools Grant Coke Exclusive Rights," *Marketing News, Marketing Perspective,* Oct. 13, 1997, 9.

45. South Carolina Nutrition Action Committee, "Soft Drinks and School-Age Children: Trends, Effects, Solutions," July 2002. Online

at www.asu.edu/educ/epsl/CERU/Articles/CERU-0203-41-OWI.pdf (retrieved March 8, 2005).

46. Kaufman, "Pop Culture."

47. Richard Salit and Celeste Tarricone, "Soda Wars: Coke, Pepsi Pay Big for Sole Rights to Sell Soft Drinks in Schools," (Providence, RI) *Journal-Bulletin,* March 14, 1999, 1A.

48. Pete Lewis, "Corporate Sponsors Help with Financing; Funding for Denver, Colorado Public Schools," *Denver Business Journal,* November 20, 1998, 6B.

49. U.S. General Accounting Office, "U.S. Public Education: Commercial Activities in Schools," (GAO/HEHS-00–156) Washington, DC, September 8, 2000.

50. U.S. Government Accountability Office, "School Meal Programs: Competitive Foods Are Available in Many Schools," (GAO-04–673). Washington, DC, April 23, 2004.

51. U.S. Government Accountability Office, "School Meal Programs."

52. B. Welburn, "Vending Ban Is No Cure for Childhood Obesity," Letter to the Editor, *Education Week,* Nov. 5, 2003.

53. K. M. Brown et al., "California School Board Members' Perceptions of Factors Influencing School Nutrition Policy," *Journal of School Health* 74, 2 (February 2004): 52–58.

54. K. M. Brown et al., "California School Board."

55. U.S. Department of Agriculture, *Foods of Minimal Nutritional Value,* Food and Nutrition Service, 2001, online at www.fns.usda.gov/cnd/ Lunch/CompetitiveFoods/report_congress.htm (retrieved March 8, 2005).

56. Salit and Tarricone, "Soda Wars."

57. Janet Grafe, "Feds, State Go Sour on Sweets in Classrooms," *Gazette Enterprise,* (Guadalupe County, TX), Oct. 19, 2003.

58. Allison Barker, "Nearly 100 Schools Selling Soft Drinks to Kids," Associated Press, March 11, 2004.

59. Jennifer Bundy, "AP Interview: Richie Robb Calls Himself 'Republican with Results.'" Associated Press, March 13, 2004.

60. Associated Press, "Can't Hold Water," American Marketing Assn. *Marketing News* (Nov 25. 2002), 6. Associated Press, "Pepsi Pours Cold Water on Girl's Project," *Seattle Times,* Nov. 4, 2002, B2.

61. Gary Boyes, personal communication, Nov. 22, 2002; quoted with permission.

62. Associated Press, "Can't Hold Water" and Associated Press, "Pepsi Pours Cold Water."

63. Boyes, personal communication.
64. W. Yelverton, "Financial Pinches in Schools Call for Creative Thinking," *Tampa Tribune*, Pasco Section, Aug. 17, 2003, B2.
65. "Deny Sweet Tooth Craving for Easy Cash for Schools," *St. Petersburg Times/Pasco Times*, Jan. 27, 2004, 2.
66. Allison Bruce, "Charleston Schools Go Pepsi Only."
67. Bruce, "Charleston Schools Go Pepsi Only."
68. Allison Bruce, "Schools' Pepsi Deal Upsets Some Parents," *Post and Courier* (Charleston, SC), Sept. 5, 2002, 1B.
69. Seanna Adcox, "School Drink Machines at Center of Health Debate."
70. Kristin King, "Norfolk Schools Vend Only Coke in Exchange for $3.2 Million," *Virginian-Pilot* (Norfolk, VA), Aug. 29, 2002, B1.
71. Allison Bruce, "Charleston Schools Go Pepsi Only."
72. L. Ishibashi, D. Woldow, and C. Grannan, "K–12 at a Crossroads: One School's Uncanny Success with Junk-Food Ban," *San Francisco Chronicle*, April 4, 2003, online at http://www.asu.edu/educ/epsl/CERU/Articles/CERU-0304-50-OWI.doc (retrieved March 8, 2005).
73. T. Vinh, "Soft Drinks Limited for Middle-Schoolers," *Seattle Times*, July 18, 2003, B1.
74. K. Ervin, "Legal Experts Warn Seattle School Board against Renewing Coke Contract," *Seattle Times*, July 2, 2003.
75. T. Vinh, "Soft Drinks Limited."
76. T. Vinh, "Soft Drinks Limited."
77. Seattle School Board, "Seattle school board approves comprehensive suite of nutrition policies," news release, Sept. 3, 2004, online at www.seattleschools.org/area/news/x40903nr.xml (retrieved March 8, 2005).
78. More information about organizations and their use of these guidelines can be found at the CERU Web site at http://www.asu.edu/educ/epsl/CERU/CERU_Guidelines.htm (retrieved March 8, 2005).
79. "Sample Policies to Encourage Healthy Eating," National Association of State Boards of Education, (undated), online at www.nasbe.org/HealthySchools/healthy_eating.html (retrieved March 8, 2005).
80. L. Reid and A. Gedissman, "Required TV Program in Schools Encourages Poor Lifestyle Choices," *AAP News*, November 2000, online at www.aap.org/advocacy/reid1100.htm (retrieved March 8, 2005).
81. American Academy of Pediatrics, Committee on School Health, policy statement, "Soft Drinks in Schools," *Pediatrics* 113, no. 1 (January 2004): 152–54, online at http://aappolicy.aappublications.org/cgi/content/full/pediatrics;113/1/152 (retrieved March 8, 2005).

See also Susan H. Thompson, "Bubble Trouble," *Tampa Tribune* (Florida), March 16, 2004, 1.

82. Koplan, Liverman, and Kraak, *Preventing Childhood Obesity.*

83. Corrinna Hawkes, *Marketing Food to Children: The Global Regulatory Environment,* Geneva, Switzerland, World Health Organization, 2004.

84. Susan Thompson, "Bubble Trouble."

85. Thompson, "Bubble Trouble."

86. "Philadelphia Public Schools to Can Sales of Soda" *Philadelphia Inquirer,* Knight Ridder/Tribune Business News, July 9, 2003.

87. Ann Bradley, "Philadelphia Schools Ban Sale of Sodas to Students," *Education Week,* News in Brief, Feb. 11, 2004.

88. Dan Hardy, "Philadelphia Schools Express Wariness against Soda Deals," *Philadelphia Inquirer,* distributed by Knight Ridder/Tribune Business News, Jan. 22, 2004.

89. "Chicago Bans Soda Pop in Schools," Associated Press, April 21, 2004.

90. Fran Spielman and Kate N. Grossman, "Aldermen Look at Reducing Snack Food in Schools," *Chicago Sun-Times,* Oct. 2, 2003, 11.

91. Michelle Martinez, "Because It's Good for You," *Austin American-Statesman,* Aug. 20, 2003, B1.

92. Jen Sansbury, "DeKalb Education Notebook: No Soda Allowed in School Machines," *Atlanta Journal-Constitution,* Jan. 1, 2004, online at www.ajc.com/metro/content/metro/dekalb/0104/01ednotebook.html (retrieved Jan. 5, 2004).

93. Charles Kinnin, "District Eyes $29,000 'Windfall,'" *Daily Southerner,* Nov. 11, 2003, online at http://dailysoutherner.com/articles/2003/11/11/news/news2.txt (retrieved Dec. 4, 2003.)

94. "Gov. Davis Signs California Childhood Obesity Prevention Act," press release, American School Food Service Association, Sept. 22, 2003, online at www.asfsa.org/newsroom/sfsnews/casb677.asp (retrieved March 8, 2005).

95. George Stewart, "No More Junk Food to Be Sold on Tustin School Campuses," *Orange County Register/Tustin News,* Nov. 27, 2003.

96. Associated Press, "Assembly Restricts Soda Sales at Schools," *San Diego Union Tribune,* Aug. 22, 2003, A5.

97. A. Molnar, *School Commercialism, Student Health, and the Pressure to Do More with Less.* Tempe, AZ: Education Policy Studies Laboratory, Arizona State University, July, 2003.

98. Susan Thompson, "Bubble Trouble."

99. "Deny Sweet Tooth Craving for Easy Cash for Schools," *St. Petersburg Times/Pasco Times*, Jan. 27, 2004, 2.

100. D. Stepp, "Schools' Vending Snacks Spared; Cherokee Board Sees Need of Cash," *Atlanta Journal-Constitution*, Feb. 6, 2004, C10.

101. Allison Bruce, "What's for Lunch?" *Post and Courier* (Charleston, SC), Aug. 12, 2003, 1C.

102. E. Doran, "Build a Better Slingshot," *Post-Standard* (Syracuse, NY), Oct. 30, 2003.

103. "Soda in Schools—New State Ruling," press release by American Quality Beverages, March 10, 2004, online at http://www.asu.edu/educ/epsl/CERU/Community%20Corner/CERU-0404-204-RCC.doc (retrieved March 8, 2005).

104. Ross Getman, Esq., attorney for AQB, personal communication, Dec. 10, 2004.

105. "Complaint for Injunctive and Declaratory Relief," Circuit Court for the State of Oregon, April 2003, online at www.commercialalert.org/orcomplaint.pdf (retrieved March 8, 2005).

106. T. Vinh, "Soft Drinks Limited."

107. Dale Buss, "Is the food industry the problem or the solution?" *New York Times*, Section 5, Aug. 29, 2004, 3.

108. Buss, "Is the food industry the problem or the solution?"

109. S. Leith, "Coke reworks pitch in schools," *Atlanta Journal-Constitution*, Nov. 15, 2003, 1A.

110. Coca-Cola Inc. "Your Power to Choose: Model Guidelines for School–Beverage Partnerships," 2003, online at http://www.asu.edu/educ/epsl/CERU/Community%20Corner/CERU-0311-180-RCC.pdf (retrieved March 8, 2005).

111. Coca-Cola Inc. "Your Power to Choose."

112. Chad Terhune, "Coke's Guidelines for Soft Drinks in Schools Face Some Criticism," *Wall Street Journal*, Nov. 17, 2003.

113. Dale Buss, "Is the food industry the problem or the solution?"

114. John F. Banzhaf III, "Eat at McDonald's, Work out All Day: Ronald Deceiving Kids in Classrooms," January 28, 2005, online at http://www.asu.edu/educ/epsl/CERU/Articles/CERU-0501-105-OWI.pdf (retrieved March 3, 2005).

115. Banzhaf, "Eat at McDonald's."

116. Banzhaf, "Eat at McDonald's."

117. Caroline Grannan, "Industry Claims Kids Don't Drink Much Soda."

118. Grannan, "Industry Claims Kids Don't Drink Much Soda."

119. Dale Buss, "Is the food industry the problem or the solution?"

120. Buss, "Is the food industry the problem or the solution?"

121. A. Molnar, D. Garcia, J. Joanu, C. Sullivan, B. McEvoy, & E. Griffin, Profiles of For-Profit Education Management Companies: Seventh Annual Report 2004–2005. Tempe, AZ: Education Policy Studies Laboratory, Education Policy Research Unit and Commercialism in Education Research Unit, March 2005, online at http://www.asu.edu/educ/epsl/CERU/Documents/EPSL-0503-101-CERU.pdf

122. Marion Nestle, *Food Politics: How the Food Industry Influences Nutrition and Health* (Berkeley, CA: University of California Press, 2002); and Marion Nestle, *Safe Food: Bacteria, Biotechnology, and Bioterrorism* (Berkeley, CA: University of California Press, 2003).

123. Marion Nestle, "Fight on Obesity Faces Hefty Commercial Problems," *Newsday* (New York), June 22, 2000, online at www.commercialalert.org/ obesitynestle.htm (retrieved March 8, 2005).

124. Irene Cherkassky, "Getting the Exclusive," *Beverage World*, October 1998, 96.

NOTES TO CHAPTER 4

1. George McGovern makes this point in an interview with Bill Moyers in "The Image Makers," A Walk Through the Twentieth Century with Bill Moyers, Corporation for Entertainment & Learning, 1984. Distributed by PBS.

2. The overall discussion of Lee's work is drawn from "The Image Makers," A Walk Through the Twentieth Century with Bill Moyers, Corporation for Entertainment & Learning, 1984. Distributed by PBS.

3. Russell Jacoby, *The Last Intellectuals: American Culture in the Age of Academe,* New York: The Noonday Press, 1989, 38.

4. Edward L. Bernays, *Crystallizing Public Opinion,* New York: Liveright Publishing Corporation, 1923.

5. Edward L. Bernays, *Propaganda,* New York: Liveright Publishing Corporation, 1928.

6. Edward L. Bernays, ed., *The Engineering of Consent,* Norman, OK: University of Oklahoma Press, 1955.

7. Edward L. Bernays, *Biography of an Idea: Memoirs of Public Relations Counsel,* New York: Simon and Schuster, 1965.

8. Bernays, *Propaganda.*

9. Bernays, *Propaganda.*

10. Bernays, *Propaganda,* 9.

11. Bernays, *Propaganda*, 11.
12. Bernays, *Propaganda*, 11.
13. Bernays, *Propaganda*, 19.
14. Bernays, *Propaganda*, 19.
15. Stuart Ewen, *Captains of Consciousness: Advertising and the Social Roots of the Consumer Culture*, New York: McGraw-Hill, 1977, 52.
16. Ewen, *The Captains of Consciousness*, 54.
17. Ewen, *The Captains of Consciousness*, 54.
18. Ewen, *The Captains of Consciousness*, 55.
19. Otis Pease, *The Responsibilities of American Advertising: Private Control and Public Influence, 1920–1940*, New Haven, CT: Yale University Press, 1958.
20. Pease, *The Responsibilities of American Advertising*, 201–202.
21. Stuart Ewen and Elizabeth Ewen, *Channels of Desire: Mass Images and the Shaping of American Consciousness*, New York: McGraw-Hill, 1982, 263–66.
22. Ewen and Ewen, *Channels of Desire*, 229.
23. Ewen and Ewen, *Channels of Desire*, 74–75.
24. Vance Packard, *The Hidden Persuaders*, New York: Pocket Books, 1963, 223.
25. David Riesman, Nathan Glazer, and Reuel Denney, *The Lonely Crowd: A Study of Changing American Character*, Garden City, NY: Doubleday, 1955.
26. John Dewey, *Experience and Education*, New York: Collier Books, 1965, 18.
27. Dewey, *Experience and Education*, 25.
28. Dewey, *Experience and Education*, 26.
29. Dewey, *Experience and Education*, 64–65.
30. Dewey, *Experience and Education*, 68–69.
31. Dewey, *Experience and Education*, 61.
32. Dewey, *Experience and Education*, 36.
33. Dewey, *Experience and Education*, 39.
34. Dewey, *Experience and Education*, 82.
35. Dewey, *Experience and Education*, 39.
36. Dewey, *Experience and Education*, 44–45.
37. Leslie Savan, *The Sponsored Life: Ads, TV, and American Culture*, Philadelphia: Temple University Press, 1994, 1.
38. Gerald Bracey, "Knowledge Universe and Virtual Schools: Educational Breakthrough or Digital Raid on the Public Treasury?" Tempe, AZ:

Arizona State University, Education Policy Studies Laboratory, online at www.asu.edu/educ/epsl/EPRU/documents/EPSL-0404–118-EPRU.doc.

39. Susan Faludi, New York: William Morrow and Co., 1999.
40. Robert H. Frank, New York: The Free Press, 1999.
41. Jean Kilbourne, New York: The Free Press, 1999.
42. John De Graaf, David Wann, and Thomas H. Naylor, San Francisco: Berrett-Koehler, 2001.
43. Juliet B. Schor, New York: Basic Books, 1998.
44. Roy F. Fox, Westport, CT: Greenwood Publishing Group, 1996.
45. Shirley R. Steinberg and Joe L. Kincheloe, eds., Boulder, CO: Westview Press, 1997.
46. Susan Linn, *Consuming Kids: The Hostile Takeover of Childhood,* New York: The New Press, 2004.
47. Jane Kenway and Elizabeth Bullen, Buckingham and Philadelphia: Open University Press, 2002.
48. Alex Molnar, Boulder, CO: Westview/HarperCollins, 1996.
49. Deron Boyles, New York: Garland Publishing, 1998.
50. William E. Doll, "Ghosts and the Curriculum," in *Curriculum Visions,* edited by William E. Doll and Noel Gough. New York: Peter Lang Publishing, 2002.
51. Matthew Klein, "School Daze," *Marketing Tools,* September 1997, 16.
52. Dave Ross and Charles Osgood, "Schools Being Named after Dead People Is a Luxury Cash-Strapped Public Schools Can No Longer Afford," CBS News Transcripts, April 19, 2004.
53. Scott Parks, "Fee to Former Superintendent Raises Issues," *Dallas Morning News,* Sept. 7, 2004.
54. Gabe Pressman, New York City Schools Chancellor Joel Klein interview, WNBC TV News Forum (transcript), March 21, 2004.
55. Gabe Pressman, New York City Schools Chancellor Joel Klein interview.
56. Andrew Wolf, "I'd Like to Buy the World a . . . Snapple?" *New York Sun,* Nov. 21, 2003, 9.
57. A. Molnar, D. Garcia, J. Joanu, C. Sullivan, B. McEvoy, & E. Griffin, Profiles of For-Profit Education Management Companies: Seventh Annual Report 2004–2005. Tempe, AZ: Education Policy Studies Laboratory, Education Policy Research Unit and Commercialism in Education Research Unit, March 2005 online at http://www.asu.edu/educ/epsl/CERU/Documents/EPSL-0503-101-CERU.pdf.

NOTES TO CHAPTER 5

1. For an excellent brief history of Edison, and an analysis of the policy implications raised by the company, see:
   Kenneth J. Saltman, *The Edison Schools: Corporate Schooling and the Assault on Public Education* (New York: Routledge, 2005).

2. "Accept 'enlightened commercialism' and get 'high-tech educational tools,' communications entrepreneur advises," *TEA News* 21, no. 5 (November 1989): 6.

3. Debra Kaufman, "Channel One Outlasts Its Critics; In-School Commercials Remain a Sore Point for Opposition," *Television Week*, Nov. 24, 2003, 18.

4. Patrick M. Reilly, "Whittle's Sale of Channel One Completed by K-III," *Wall Street Journal*, Oct. 3, 1994.

5. Gerald Bracey, "The Market in Theory Meets the Market in Practice: The Case of Edison Schools," Tempe, AZ: Arizona State University Education Policy Studies Laboratory, 2002.

6. Bracey, "The Market in Theory."

7. John S. Friedman, "Big Business Goes to School," *The Nation* 254, no. 6 (Feb. 17, 1991): 188–92.

8. Deborah Sontag, "Yale President Quitting to Lead National Private School System," *New York Times*, May 26, 1992, A1.

9. Tom McNichol, "Chris Whittle's Big Test," *USA Weekend*, Sept. 18–20, 1992; Jesse Kornbluth, "Chris and Benno's Excellent Adventure," *Vanity Fair*, August 1992, 147; Carol Jouzaitis, "Preppy Pitchman," *Chicago Tribune*, Sept. 17, 1992.

10. Patrick M. Reilly and Suzanne Alexander, "Whittle's Plan for Big Growth Runs into Snags," *Wall Street Journal*, Sept. 10, 1992.

11. Joe Nathan, *Charter Schools: Creating Hope and Opportunity for American Education*, San Francisco: Jossey Bass, 1996, xxvii.

12. "Ruling allows tax money to go to religious schools," CNN, June 11, 1998, online at www.cnn.com/US/9806/11/school.choice/ (retrieved March 4, 2005).

13. "Supreme Court affirms school voucher program," June 27, 2002, online at archives.cnn.com/2002/LAW/06/27/scotus.school.vouchers/ (retrieved March 4, 2005).

14. William Booth and Rene Sanchez, "Drug Reform Initiatives Receive Support of Voters; Gun Control also Popular; School Vouchers Not Embraced," *Washington Post*, Nov. 9, 2000, A48.

15. Vouchers hit dead end (undated), People for the American Way, online at www.pfaw.org/pfaw/general/default.aspx?oid=16044 (retrieved Nov. 29, 2004).

16. "About Voucher Programs," palmbeachpost.com Voucher News Archive, online at www.palmbeachpost.com/news/content/news/vouchers/archive.html (retrieved March 9, 2005).

17. "About Voucher Programs," palmbeachpost.com.

18. Mindy Sink, "Voucher Law Unconstitutional," *New York Times*, June 29, 2004, A22.

19. Spencer S. Hsu and Justin Blum, "D.C. School Vouchers Win Final Approval," *Washington Post*, Jan. 23, 2004, A1.

20. Charter schools (undated), Center for Education Reform, online at www.edreform.com/index.cfm?fuseAction=stateStatsandpSectionID=15andcSectionID=44 (retrieved March 3, 2005).

21. Historical stock quotes and charts, MarketWatch BigCharts, online at bigcharts.marketwatch.com/historical/default.asp?detect=1&symbol=EDSN&close_date=2%2F8%2F2001&x=18&y=27 (retrieved March 9, 2005).

22. Mark Walsh, "San Francisco Moves to Revoke Edison's Contract," *Education Week* 20, no. 29 (April 4, 2001): 12.
    Peggy Walsh-Sarnecki, "Report Criticizes Charter Schools," *Detroit Free Press*, Oct. 24, 2000.

23. For one example among many, see Caroline Grannan, "Most Edison Schools in Illinois Suffer Drops in Test Scores," San Francisco, Parents Advocating School Accountability, Feb. 17, 2002, online at http://pasaorg.tripod.com/edison/pdfs/Illinois.pdf (retrieved Nov. 29, 2004).

24. Diane Brady, "Commentary: Chris Whittle's New IPO Deserves a D-minus," *Business Week,* Sept. 6, 1999.

25. Gerald Bracey, "The Market in Theory Meets the Market in Practice: The Case of Edison Schools," Tempe, AZ: Arizona State University Education Policy Studies Laboratory, 2002.

26. David B. Caruso, "State Auditor Says Contract for Edison Study of Philadelphia Schools Was Awarded Improperly," Associated Press, Aug. 21, 2002.

27. "Pennsylvania Auditor General Casey Audit Exposes Details," press release distributed by PR Newswire for the Pennsylvania Dept. of the Auditor General, Nov. 20, 2002.

28. Ovetta Wiggins and Dale Mezzacappa, "Pennsylvania Education Secretary Resigns," *Philadelphia Inquirer,* Dec. 18, 2002, B2.

29. "Resigning State Education Chief Moves to Oust School Board in Chester," Associated Press, Jan. 4, 2003.

30. Susan Snyder, "Private Firm Hired to Help Save Phila. Schools," *Philadelphia Inquirer*, Aug. 2, 2001, A1.

31. Jacques Steinberg, "In Largest Schools Takeover, State Will Run Philadelphia's," *New York Times*, Dec. 22, 2001, A1.

    Jacques Steinberg, "Private Groups Get 42 Schools In Philadelphia," *New York Times*, April 18, 2002, A1.

    "Philly Contract Says Edison Schools Can Be Fired for Any Reason," Associated Press, Aug. 27, 2002.

32. William Bunch, "Stock in Edison Schools Rose on News of City Deal," *Philadelphia Inquirer*, Aug. 3, 2001, A9.

33. Martha Woodall, "Of Philadelphia Schools or Edison, Who's Really Saving Whom?" *Philadelphia Inquirer*, Aug. 19, 2001, C1.

34. Dale Mezzacappa, "Edison Schools Lays Off Aides, Secretaries in Philadelphia," *Philadelphia Inquirer*, Aug. 28, 2002, B3.

35. "Edison Returns Supplies for Its 20 Philadelphia Schools," Associated Press, Aug. 30, 2002.

36. Dale Mezzacappa, "Edison Schools Says Test System Surmounts Obstacles," *Philadelphia Inquirer*, Dec. 18, 2002, B1.

37. Mezzacappa, "Edison Schools Says Test System Surmounts Obstacles."

38. "Playground Construction to Start," *Times-Union*, March 31, 2003, B3.

39. David B. Caruso, "For-Profit Education Firm Says It Outperforms Public Schools," Associated Press, March 1, 2003.

40. "Edison Schools Reports Strong Achievement Gain," press release distributed by PR Newswire for Edison Schools Inc., Dec. 23, 2002.

    "Edison Schools in Baltimore Continues to Improve on Standardized Test," press release distributed by PR Newswire for Edison Schools Inc., Dec. 9, 2002.

41. David B. Caruso, "For-Profit Education Firm Says It Outperforms Public Schools," Associated Press, March 1, 2003.

42. Dan Hardy, "Student Test Scores Drop in Pennsylvania Schools Run by Edison," *Philadelphia Inquirer*, Oct. 16, 2002.

43. "Edison Schools in Pennsylvania Post Strong Academic Gains on State Assessment," press release distributed by PR Newswire for Edison Schools, Oct. 16, 2002.

44. Robert L. White, "Charter School Is Not Outperforming Arbor Hill Neighbor," letter to the editor, *Times-Union* (Albany, NY), July 25, 2004, A6.

45. "GAO Discounts Interest Group-Backed Studies of Edison Schools," press release distributed by PR Newswire for Edison Schools, Oct. 30, 2002.

   Michael Rubinkam, "GAO: 'Insufficient' Data to Grade Private Education Companies," Associated Press, Oct. 30, 2002.

46. "Michigan Edison Schools Post Strong Academic Gains on MEAP," press release for Edison Schools distributed by PR Newswire, May 18, 2004.

47. Miriam Hill, "This School Year Is Do or Die for Edison," *Philadelphia Inquirer*, Oct. 2, 2002.

48. Tawnell Hobbs, "DISD Rejects Edison Contract," *Dallas Morning News*, Aug. 23, 2002, 31A.

49. Lisa Kim Bach, "'Micromanagement Issues': School officials Greet Bills with Skepticism," *Las Vegas Review-Journal*, March 27, 2003, 7B.

50. "Former Edison Schools Improve under Wichita District Leadership," Associated Press, May 27, 2003.

51. Diana Jean Schemo, "Nation's Charter Schools Lagging behind, U.S. Test Scores Reveal," *New York Times*, Aug. 17, 2004, A1.

52. Sam Dillon and Diana Jean Schemo, "Charter Schools Fall Short in Public Schools Matchup," *New York Times*, Nov. 23, 2004, A21.

   Kara Finnegan et al., *Evaluation of the Public Charter Schools Program*, Washington, DC: SRI International, 2004; U.S. Department of Education, doc # 2004–08, online at www.ed.gov/rschstat/eval/choice/pcsp-final/finalreport.pdf (retrieved Nov. 23, 2004).

53. Dillon and Schemo, "Charter Schools Fall Short."

54. Dillon and Schemo, "Charter Schools Fall Short."

55. Jay P. Greene and Greg Forster, *The Teachability Index: Can Disadvantaged Students Learn?* New York, The Manhattan Institute, Education Working Paper No. 6, September 2004, online at www.manhattan-institute.org/html/ewp_06.htm (retrieved Dec. 6, 2004).

56. Leah Friedman, "Southeast Asks Board to Approve Attendance Incentive Program," *State Journal Register* (Springfield, IL), July 23, 2003, 9.

57. "Contingency Plans," *Vancouver Sun*, Aug. 9, 2002, F4.

   "Edison Schools to Flint: We Aren't Going Broke," Associated Press, Oct. 23, 2002.

58. Rick Karlin, "School Confronts Financial Concerns," *Times Union* (Albany, NY), Oct. 23, 2002, B1.

59. Liz Bowie, "Edison Tries to Reassure State Board of Education," *Baltimore Sun*, Oct. 30, 2002, 1B.

60. "Philadelphia Schools Move to Shield Property in Case of Edison Bankruptcy," *Philadelphia Inquirer,* Oct. 2, 2002.

61. William C. Smith, "Edison GC Schooled in and out of Class," *National Law Journal* 25, no. 66 (Dec. 23, 2002): A16.

62. Claude Solnik, "PricewaterhouseCoopers Pulled into Suits with Embattled Edison Schools," *Long Island Business News,* Dec. 27, 2002.

63. Ricki Fulman, "SEIU Opposes Privatization," *Pensions and Investments,* Jan. 6, 2003, 8.
      Ken MacFadyen, "Leeds Weld Completes First Deal from Fund. *BuyOuts,*" March 3, 2003.

64. "Investor Pulls out of Edison," *York Daily Record,* Aug. 14, 2003, A2.

65. Brian O'Reilly, "Why Edison Doesn't Work," *Fortune,* Dec. 9, 2002, 148.

66. O'Reilly, "Why Edison Doesn't Work."

67. O'Reilly, "Why Edison Doesn't Work."

68. "Order Needed in Problematic School District," *Delaware County Daily Times,* Nov. 29, 2004, online at www.zwire.com/site/news.cfm?BRD=1675&dept_id=18168&newsid=13453109&PAG=461&rfi=9 (retrieved Nov. 29, 2004).
      See also Dan Hardy, "Student Test Scores Drop in Pennsylvania Schools Run by Edison," *Philadelphia Inquirer,* Oct. 16, 2002.

69. Hardy, "Student Test Scores Drop."

70. David B. Caruso, "After Years of Losses, Edison Schools Starts Demanding Steeper Fees," Associated Press, Aug. 21, 2002.

71. Miriam Hill, "This School Year Is Do or Die for Edison," *Philadelphia Inquirer,* Oct. 2, 2002.

72. "Chester Needs School System That Works," *Delaware County Daily Times,* July 2, 2004, online at www.zwire.com/site/news.cfm?newsid=12183843&BRD=1675&PAG=461&dept_id=18168&rfi=6 (retrieved July 10, 2004).

73. Josh Cornfield, "Chester Upland Putting Sale Signs on Properties," *Delaware County Daily Times,* Oct. 29, 2004, online at http://delcotimes.com/site/news.cfm?newsid=13249702&BRD=1675&PAG=461&dept_id=18171&rfi=6 (retrieved Oct. 29, 2004).

74. "Order Needed in Problematic School District," *Delaware County Daily Times,* Nov. 29, 2004, online at www.zwire.com/site/news.cfm?BRD=1675&dept_id=18168&newsid=13453109&PAG=461&rfi=9 (retrieved Nov. 29, 2004).
      Dale Mezzacappa, "District Chief Urges Edison's Departure," *Philadelphia Inquirer,* Feb. 16, 2005, B1.

75. "In Brief," *Investor's Business Daily*, Dec. 31, 2002, A2.

"Edison Schools Reports Significant Improvements," press release distributed by PR Newswire for Edison Schools, May 13, 2003.

76. Martha Woodall, "Edison Schools in Default on Loans," *Philadelphia Inquirer*, May 23, 2003.

77. Diana B. Henriques, "Edison Schools' Founder to Take It Private," *New York Times*, July 15, 2003.

78. David B. Caruso, "Edison Founder to Take Company Private," Associated Press, July 15, 2003.

79. Marianne D. Hurst, "Fla. Teachers Riled by Edison Deal," *Education Week*, Oct. 8. 2003.

80. "Wechsler Harwood Sues on Behalf of Holders of Class A Shares of Common Stock of Edison Schools Inc.," press release distributed for Wechsler Harwood LLP by PrimeZone Media Network, July 15, 2003.

See also "Retail Sales Show Life," *Washington Post*, July 16, 2003, E2.

81. See http://securities.stanford.edu/1024/EDSN02–01/20040719_0015_023692.pdf (retrieved Dec. 10, 2004).

82. Diane B. Henriques, "Edison Stays Afloat by Altering Course," *New York Times*, July 3, 2003, C1.

83. See   www.edisonschools.com/overview/alliance.html   (retrieved March 8, 2005).

"Edison Schools to Serve More Than 250,000 Students in 2004–2005," press release, Sept. 20, 2004, posted on Edison Schools Inc., corporate Web site, online at www.edisonschools.com/news/news.cfm?ID=174 (retrieved Nov. 29, 2004).

84. Anne Wujcik, "Edison Plans to Exploit NCLB Funding," *Heller Report on Educational Technology Markets* 14, No. 3 (Jan. 1, 2003), 3.

85. David B. Caruso, "Firms See Potential Windfall in Education Reform," Associated Press, Nov. 30, 2002.

86. David A. Lieb, "Education Officials Pan Summer School Proposal," Associated Press, April 1, 2003.

87. See www.zoomerang.com/recipient/survey.zgi?p=WEB2MJVVSQUA (retrieved Nov. 29, 2004).

88. The material on the growth and evolution of various for-profit education management companies is, unless otherwise noted, drawn from the following reports:

A. Molnar, G. Wilson, and D. Allen, *Profiles of For-Profit Education Management Companies 2002–2003*, Tempe, AZ: Education Policy Studies Laboratory, Education Policy Research Unit, January 2003, online at www.asu.edu/educ/epsl/CERU/Documents/EPSL-0301–102-CERU.pdf.

A. Molnar, G. Wilson, and D. Allen, *Profiles of For-Profit Education Management Companies 2003–2004.* Tempe, AZ: Education Policy Studies Laboratory, Education Policy Research Unit, February 2004, online at www.asu.edu/educ/epsl/CERU/Documents/EPSL-0402–101-CERU.pdf.

A. Molnar, et al., unpublished data collected for *Profiles of For-Profit Education Management Companies, 2004–2005,* Tempe, AZ: Education Policy Studies Laboratory, Education Policy Research Unit, March 2005.

89. A. Molnar, G. Wilson, and D. Allen, *Profiles of For-Profit Education Management Companies 2002–2003.*

A. Molnar, G. Wilson, and D. Allen, *Profiles of For-Profit Education Management Companies 2003–2004.*

A. Molnar, et al., unpublished data collected for *Profiles of For-Profit Education Management Companies, 2004–2005.*

90. A. Molnar, G. Wilson, and D. Allen, *Profiles of For-Profit Education Management Companies 2003–2004.*

91. Claire Luna, "Home Cyber Schools, and Critics, Growing," *Los Angeles Times,* part 2, Jan. 6, 2003, 1.

92. "Cyber Schools Fill a Niche for Parents, Kids," *Chicago Tribune,* Dec. 1, 2002.

93. "Online K-8 Schools Growing," *Instructor* 112, no. 6 (March 1, 2003), 16.

94. Mary Lord, "O E-pioneers!" *U.S. News and World Report* 133, no. 22 (Dec. 9, 2002), 56.

95. "Districts Opening Online Charter Schools around Ohio," Associated Press, March 17, 2003.

96. Anne Davis, "Wisconsin's Cyber Schools Testing the Waters," *Milwaukee Journal Sentinel,* March 1, 2003.

97. Educate Inc. press release, July 1, 2003, online at www.educate-inc.com/pdfs/SYLVAN_K-12_BUSINESS_UNITS_ACQUIRED_BY_EDUCATE_INC_TODAY.pdf (retrieved May 6, 2004).

Educate proposed IPO filing, May 14, 2004, online at www.sec.gov/Archives/edgar/data/1286862/000119312504088499/ds1.htm (retrieved May 19, 2004).

98. "Chancellor Arizona Connections Academy Receives Approval to Open 'School without Walls,'" press release distributed for Chancellor Arizona Connections Academy (CA2) by PR Newswire, July 16, 2003.

99. "State Board OKs Five New Electronic Schools for Students in Kindergarten through 12th Grade," Associated Press, July 16, 2003.

100. Tyson Freeman, "Bennett-Led Startup Gets $20M," *Daily News* (New York, NY), April 3, 2003.

101. Andrew Trotter, "'Virtual School' Battle Sparks Minn. Lawsuit," *Education Week,* Oct. 29, 2003.

102. "California Virtual Academies to Host 'Innovation in Education Expo,'" press release distributed by U.S. Newswire for K12 Inc., March 25, 2003.

   See also "Idaho Virtual Academy to Host 'Innovation in Education Expo,'" press release distributed by U.S. Newswire for K12 Inc., March 20, 2003.

103. Anne Davis, "Northern Ozaukee Unanimously OKs Virtual School Deal," *Milwaukee Journal Sentinel,* March 11, 2003, 1B.

104. "K12 (Again!) and others who covet homeschoolers and why." (Undated) Ohio Home Education Coalition Web site. Retrieved 3/15/04 from http://www.homeschoolfreedom.org/k12again.shtml

105. Maria T. Welych, "Central New York Doesn't Foster Cyberschools," *Post-Standard* (Syracuse, NY), Jan. 15, 2003, C6.

106. Karen Arenson, "Virtual Charter School Is Rejected," *New York Times,*" Dec. 18, 2002, B13.

107. John Hildebrand, "How a Cyberschool Got Knocked Offline," *Newsday* (NY), Jan. 7, 2003, A20.

108. Hildebrand, "How a Cyberschool Got Knocked Offline."

109. Luis Huerta, "Losing Public Accountability: A Home-schooling Charter," in Bruce Fuller, ed. *Inside Charter Schools: The Paradox of Radical Decentralization.* (Cambridge: Harvard University Press, 2000).

110. Gerald Bracey, "Knowledge Universe and Virtual Schools: Educational Breakthrough or Digital Raid on the Public Treasury?" Tempe, AZ: Education Policy Studies Laboratory, April 2004, online at www.asu.edu/educ/epsl/EPRU/documents/EPSL-0404–118-EPRU.doc (retrieved March 4, 2005).

111. Andrew Trotter, "'Virtual School' Battle Sparks Minn. Lawsuit," *Education Week,* Oct. 29, 2003.

   Robert C. Johnston, "Wisconsin Teachers Sue to Close Online School," *Education Week,* Jan. 21, 2004.

112. Trotter, "'Virtual School' Battle Sparks Minn. Lawsuit."

113. Trotter, "'Virtual School' Battle Sparks Minn. Lawsuit."

114. Johnston, "Wisconsin Teachers Sue."

115. Johnston, "Wisconsin Teachers Sue."

116. Adam Wilson, "Group Takes Aim at Schroeder with Poll," *Lewiston Morning Tribune* (Idaho), May 19, 2004, 5A.

117. Jim Fisher, "More Idahoans Deserve Private Education Payoffs," *Lewiston Morning Tribune* (Idaho), May 30, 2004, 1F.

118. Bridget Gutierrez, "Cyber Education Finds Supporters," *San Antonio Express-News*, April 27, 2003, 1B.

119. Janet Elliott and Polly Ross Hughes, "Home-School Bills Have Mixed Day," *Houston Chronicle*, April 24, 2003, A29.

120. Andrea Coombes, "Online classes: A powerful K–12 educational supplement," CBS.MarketWatch.com, April 8, 2003.

121. Coombes, "Online classes."

122. Susan Ohanian, "The K12 Virtual Primary School History Curriculum: A Participant's-Eye View," Tempe, AZ: Educational Policy Studies Laboratory, April 2004, 2–3.

123. Ohanian, "The K12 Virtual Primary School History Curriculum."

124. Andrew Trotter, "Bennett's Online System Needs Work, Critic Contends," *Education Week,* May 30, 2001.

125. Bonnie Rothman Morris, "Home School in Cyberspace," *New York Times,* May 29, 2003.

126. Lord, "O E-pioneers!"

127. Rhea Borja, "U.S. Audit Raps Arizona's Use of Charter Aid," *Education Week*, Dec. 3, 2003.

128. John Gehring, "E. D. Steers Grants to Pro-Privatization Groups, Report Charges," *Education Week*, Dec. 3, 2003.

129. Jeff Archer, "Private Charter Managers Team Up," *Education Week*, Feb. 4, 2004.

NOTES TO CHAPTER 6

1. C. Grannan, "Edison School's Publicity Misstated Scores," press release distributed by Parents Advocating School Accountability, Sept. 2, 2002, online at http://pasaorg.tripod.com/edison/pdfs/morelies.pdf (retrieved March 10, 2004).

2. C. Grannan, "Rand Denies Link with Questionable Edison Success Claim," press release distributed by Parents Advocating School Accountability, June 14, 2002, online at http://pasaorg.tripod.com/edison/pdfs/RAND.pdf (retrieved March 10, 2005).

3. H. Greenberg, "Lessons on Profitability (or the Lack Thereof) from Edison Schools," TheStreet.com, June 6, 2000, online at

www.thestreet.com/comment/herbonthestreet/953644.html (retrieved March 4, 2005).

4. Wilson, personal curriculum vitae.

5. "Panel Backs Bonds for Charter School," *Milwaukee Journal Sentinel*, Feb. 16, 2001.

6. D. Oplinger and D. Willard, "David Brennan's White Hat Management Changes the Way Business, Politics, and School Vouchers Mix," *Akron Beacon Journal*, Dec. 13, 1999.

7. Anne Wujcik, "Edison Plans to Exploit NCLB Funding," *Heller Report on Educational Technology Markets* 14, no. 3 (Jan. 1, 2003): 3.

8. "Edison Schools to Serve More Than 250,000 Students in 2004–2005," Sept. 20, 2004, Edison Schools Inc., corporate Web site, online at www.edisonschools.com/news/news.cfm?ID=174 (retrieved Nov. 29, 2004).

9. Alec McGillis, "Pitching the Quick Fix," *Baltimore Sun*, Sept. 19, 2004.

10. McGillis, "Pitching the quick fix."

11. Robert Brumfeld, "High-Stakes Cheating Spawns New Market," eSchool News, March 9, 2005, online at http://www.eschoolnews.com/news/pfshowStory.cfm?ArticleID=5564 (retrieved March 9, 2005).

12. Sarah Fenske, Eating It Up: Are HISD and Aramark Cooking the Books to Feast on Federal Breakfast Subsidies? *Houston Press*, Nov. 4, 2004, online at /www.houstonpress.com/issues/2004-11-04/news.html (retrieved Nov. 11, 2004).

13. Stephanie Banchero, "Schools Told to Outsource Tutoring," *Chicago Tribune*, Dec. 9, 2004, 1.

14. "In Need of a Tutorial on Tutoring," *Chicago Tribune*, Dec. 12, 2004, 8.

15. Tracy Dell'Angela and Jodi S. Cohen, "Tutoring Firm Expelled from Seven of City's Schools," *Chicago Tribune*, March 7, 2005, 1.

16. Dell'Angela and Cohen, "Tutoring Firm Expelled."

17. Dell'Angela and Cohen, "Tutoring Firm Expelled."

18. "In Need of a Tutorial on Tutoring," *Chicago Tribune*.

19. Jodi S. Cohen and Tracy Dell'Angela, "U.S. Tutor Initiative Is Itself Left Behind," *Chicago Tribune*, Dec. 18, 2004, 1.

20. Association of Community Organizations for Reform Now and American Institute for Social Justice, "Accountability Left Behind—While Children and Schools Face High Stakes Testing, Tutoring Companies Get a Free Ride," Washington, DC and Dallas, TX: Authors, 2004.

21. Association of Community Organizations for Reform Now and American Institute for Social Justice, "Accountability Left Behind."

22. Association of Community Organizations for Reform Now and American Institute for Social Justice, "Accountability Left Behind."

23. Association of Community Organizations for Reform Now and American Institute for Social Justice, "Accountability Left Behind."

24. J. Reaves, "From Public Good to Private Privilege," unpublished manuscript, Arizona State University, Education Policy Studies Laboratory, 2002.

25. Press Kit, World Education Market, May 24–27, 2000, Vancouver Trade and Centre, British Columbia, Canada. Quoted in Wayne Nelles, "The World Education Market Comes to Canada: Competition in a Two Trillion Dollar Global 'Industry.' " In *Our Schools, Our Selves* 10 (2) (#62) (January 2001): 93.

26. Maud Barlow, "The Last Frontier—Explaining GATS," *The Ecologist*, Jan. 22, 2001, online at www.theecologist.org/archive_article.html?article= 151&category=55 (retrieved Jan. 6, 2004).

27. Press Kit, World Education Market. See also Cynthia Guttman, "Education: The Last Frontier for Profit," *UNESCO Courier*, online at www.unesco.org/courier/2000_11/uk/dosso.htm (retrieved Jan. 6, 2004).

28. World Trade Organization, General Agreement on Trade in Services, April 1, 1994, 286, online at www.wto.org/english/docs_e/legal_e/ 26-gats.pdf (retrieved Jan. 6, 2004).

29. Consumers International, "The General Agreement on Trade in Services: An Impact Assessment by Consumers International," London: Author, 2001, online at www.consumersinternational.org/publications/ full_serv.pdf (retrieved Jan. 6, 2004).

30. Consumers International, "The General Agreement on Trade in Services."

31. G. Rikowski, "Schools and the GATS Enigma," paper presented at EPRU research seminar, Education for Profit: Private Sector Participation in Education, Nov. 27, 2002.

32. Rikowski, "Schools and the GATS enigma."

33. John Dewey, *Experience and Education* (New York: Collier Books, [1938] 1965).

INDEX